WHEN YOUR HAND IS IN THE LION'S MOUTH

WHEN YOUR HAND IS IN THE LION'S MOUTH

THE LIFE AND WISDOM OF
A MAN NAMED GREEN

Nita Whitaker

Dedication

For sweet mommy in heaven, Ola Mae Whitaker, everything I do,
I think of you and hope I am making you proud.

For my siblings, Kathy, Alene and Green Jr.,
and my amazing daughters Skye and Liisi LaFontaine,
you've all enriched and blessed my life.

But mostly for you, my dearest Daddy,
I write and dedicate this book to you and your extraordinary love.
I believe this book will be a source of inspiration
for those who will get to know you in these pages.

Thank you, Daddy.

Table of Contents

Foreword

By Anika Noni Rose
Tony Award winner and Disney's Princess Tiana

To know Green Whitaker "Poppa Green" is to love him. His eyes
sparkle with joy, spirit, and sometimes mischief. All of which he has
imbued his daughter Nita with. You can feel the love he poured into
the little girl attached to her daddy's leg, and the daughter whose
laughter is beautiful and serves humanity in the spirit of the good
Samaritan.

In the 20 plus years I've been privileged to know Poppa Green
he has never forgotten my name, (though I'm likely to be called Baby;
quite happily, I might add) or when we first met. And he has always
made me feel loved. His voice speaks to the soul of the beautiful
blackness that nourishes the South, in spite of itself. And his singing
harkens back to a style of singing of church and field that reminds me
of my southern born grandma, puts tears in my eyes, and will soon be
lost if not preserved.

The way Princess Tiana was loved and supported by her daddy
taught her how to love and value her culture and the soul of culture,
humanity. It allowed her to step out into the world assured, to discover and grasp her dreams, love, and even in the end, to her surprise,
a crown. That was a beautiful fairytale and not always the way men
of that era were taught to or allowed to love. But Poppa Green is a
real-life prince of a man who loved his wife in a warm and tactile
way, and did the same with his son and three daughters. And yes, the
youngest even worked and found her way to a crown...but that's her
story to tell.

Green is the color of nourishment, of life and growth. And
Green Whitaker has nourished his family, lived a life that though small

to some, is vast in its knowledge and experience. And through his words, actions and love, he continues to grow a family, and through his children, grandchildren, great grandchildren, and those just happy to be taken under his wing, a people who refuse to be extinguished time and time again.

I am so glad that his journey is being preserved and shared in this beautiful tribute of a man who continues to walk in love, strength, and dignity. A man whose words are worthy of hearing and learning from. A man whose hand was in the lion's mouth more often, I'm sure, than we know; but who has all ten fingers intact. A man I am honored to love.

Introduction

Whenever a friend or family member would confide in me or ask me for advice, I found myself reaching back and drawing from the same well of wisdom, quips and anecdotes that my dad tapped to help us all navigate life. He handed us stories laced with lessons and learnings. When I realized the deeper universal value of his stories how he navigated the life he was born into, his lessons and recollections, this book was born.

My dad has lived most of his life with his hand in the lion's mouth. Being born a black man in the rural south, there was always the desire for a better life and big dreams against the lion's trampling oppression of the Jim Crow era. Watching his parents and other siblings navigate a way forward to become independent of the systems that held them in a place of inferiority somehow didn't leave him bitter—it made him better. He lived through and witnessed times I've barely read about in our history books but in honoring his name and his family, he chose a divine path of growth into a man who embodies the best of us. He taught me and my siblings the ultimate lesson of loving and respecting ourselves in the pursuit of carving out our lives. This is how you pat the lion's head, and how you make a mark, and how you quietly win at being human.

Many of the stories I share in these coming pages have taken root within me; some may linger with you. They're beyond just "life lessons" or some kind of teachable moment. Sometimes they're silly, sometimes they're about his history and what he experienced; they speak to the human condition and what we can all be capable of, how we learn and grow from what life gives us, and how we can add just a little bit of kindness to the world through being loving, mindful, caring humans. The history and lessons that shaped my father, and thus my life and learning, will shape the lives of my daughters. That is immortality: how our stories become a part of who we are and then live on.

Like the sun, my dad's indomitable spirit has warmed my life. His love has been vast, unbound, and beautiful like the endless deep blue sea. This steady strong black man named Green, the father I was given, has walked into the fullness of his name over the course of his ninety-six years (and counting). With an unusual name that can be *"the color of spring, or big like a mountain, or tall like a tree"*, Green is everything his name meant for him to be.

I have worked with some of the music industry's top artists. From my undefeated Grand Champion Female Vocalist win on *Star Search*, to "birthing" some of Whitney Houston's greatest hit songs. The words and lessons my father taught made room for my musical talent to be nurtured and gave me the confidence and foundation to have worked with many of entertainment's greatest names as a respected peer. I have had the privilege of appearing on some of the world's great stages and working with top artists: I've been mentored by legendary producer, David Foster, sang duets with Andre Bocelli and Josh Groban, crooned with Michael Bublé, and worked with songwriters Carole King, Carole Bayer Sayer, Burt Bacharach, and Kenny "Babyface" Edmonds. I was influenced and taught by them all but no one I have ever met has influenced and taught me as much as my dad, Green Whitaker.

I have watched the human experience from grand stages as well as the bedside in an intensive care unit, and the view from my community and church life. Yet I deeply believe that we as a people, can learn from the simple powerful lessons of a great father. Our struggles make us whole. I don't believe fame is the only ingredient to an exceptional life but that extraordinary moments can and have come through ordinary people.

Even as a child, I knew our simple family was quite extraordinary and that our parents were exceptional people. This nourishing story of love and support, supports the child in all of us.

In a world that is often broken and hurting, we are desperate for true stories of good kind men who almost effortlessly beat the odds and leave in their wake offspring that are full of love and faith and family. I hope that these stories can serve as a reminder of all the lessons I was taught as a child: that love will always win, that we are not destined to become something simply because of our circumstances or the way we were raised, that we are not defined by what happened to us, and that with grit, humor, and faith, we can all travel together through this miraculous thing called life. The foundation of a profound fatherly love and protection, the love that made me who I am today, is what I share — and what I hope every little girl and child can have.

So with that, I share the life, wisdom, and lessons of a truly extraordinary man.

CHAPTER 1
Boy Whitaker

———————

They were married twenty-nine sweet years, but it still wasn't long enough. Is it ever long enough? My Dad, Green Whitaker, was a vibrant and healthy man when my mother died. We were in shock and disbelief that our smart, strong, healthy mother was really gone from this earth. From that eight dollars with which they started together, they had bought a little house and raised four busy bustling children in it, expanding the home as the family grew. It was a home full of love and learning, ritual and rules, music and mayhem, but most importantly, a highly functional family who loved one other. Daddy had to carry on with the four of us.

Afterward, Dad had business matters to handle and insurance issues to fight. He also had to find a way to support two children in college without Mother's much-needed second income. He was instructed to do what's called a succession, the process of settling a deceased person's estate and distributing property to their heirs. Other than his partnership in Good Samaritan Funeral home, our home was the largest and most-prized possession they shared as a couple.

Dad's birth certificate was required for the succession. After my sister made some phone calls, she was told he could pick it up at the courthouse. He drove downtown to pick up that vital piece of paper that for some reason or another he had never before needed. And that's when he saw it. Right there in black and white, where his name Green belonged, was simply the word Boy. Boy Whitaker.

Daddy had been known as Green for fifty-one years, named after his paternal grandfather who had died before he was born. He remembered sitting on his maternal grandmother's knee as a small child, looking up at her brown sun-worn skin when she rubbed his head and said to him, "I'm not gon' be 'round to see you grow up, but

I'mma leave you my charm." My dad took that name and the charm that grew even more as he became a man. Dad knew who he was and was proud of the legacy of his name. "When someone give you they name, it mean somethin'," he said.

He has attended numerous funerals, including those of all his siblings, his parents, some cousins and dear friends, nieces and nephews, and his wife. He certainly has known some sadness in his time. But this now ninety-six-year-old dignified black man, raised out of the rural red dirt of north Louisiana and born with a servant of the Lord's heart, always leaned on his faith and understood it was ordained for us to return to our Heavenly Father. I am sure there are things he saw and experienced that he never could have dreamed were possible in his lifetime, and some things he wished he could unsee, but he took in all in stride as life continued to school him and he grew more into himself.

Dad has a way with words. The way he says things either leaves you thinking or makes you giggle. His life has been lived with an innate goodness, kindness, and common sense. In his ninety-six years, he went from the plantation cotton fields of the Jim Crow South to the uprising and revelations of the Civil Rights movement and desegregation, to seeing the splendor of the vast Alaskan wilderness. Dad has cruised the deep blue waters of the Caribbean, observed the polluted skies of Beijing and the magnificent Great Wall of China, marveled at the sculpture of David in Florence and the Pieta in Rome, and relaxed on the warm beaches and poolsides of Southern California. He toured our Capitol Building in Washington D.C. and enjoyed a dinner cruise on the Potomac River. He took us kids on a road trip to Disneyworld. When I saw how beautifully clean and sparkly lit it was, I asked Daddy, "Is this what heaven would look like?"

Finally, he bore witness to Barack Obama becoming the first African-American President of the United States. Dad proclaimed, "Never thought I'd see the day!" But he did and it was a monumental moment for him to witness.

He has seen the best and worst of times and of people, the

seasons of change in what American felt like then and now, that's for sure. Somehow, he came through all of that with a soft, kind heart, and a genuine love for all people.

Some men will amass large bank accounts and portfolios, acquire real estate and land properties in their lives. Others will be famous for their talents, entrepreneurial skills, or inheritances that makes them wealthy. Dad always thought that success was good but that it was far more important to be significant. He never believed that material success alone or a fat bank account is what made a man rich. "Rich is something you feel deep in your soul and it ain't got nothin' to do with money," he said. "It's your connection to God, doing good in the world, making a difference in people's lives and to love your family. If those things line up, ain't no dollar amount in the world give you that kind of wealth or peace." He would add, "From a time where people lived off the land and worked hard long days on plantation farms to this time of smartphones and computers, times have changed but some things remain the same. Things like the way we love, the way we live, and how we treat one 'nother. I look at it all as a great journey, sometimes like a wild ride, other times like a slow-movin' river. But as the old folks say, I wouldn't take nothin' for my journey now."

Even learning and seeing that he had no name on that birth certificate didn't faze him one bit. He knew he was Green, Green Whitaker Sr., and that he was loved; that he was the expression of the love of his family, and a beloved child of God. No piece of paper was needed for that. Like the way my dad felt about his father, that Boy Whitaker grew to be a man who would be my daddy, the greatest man I have ever known.

Highway sign marking the rural community of Holly, Louisiana

CHAPTER 2
Down Home

Daddy often used the phrase "down home" when referring to his boyhood days in Holly, a small farming town in northwest Louisiana. The Whitaker family lived on an eighty-acre tract of land they owned, where they raised some farm animals, planted and harvested their own cotton, corn, fruits, and vegetables. They only bought sugar, rice, and flour; everything else they grew or farmed themselves, even syrup. Fridays were special because a treat was guaranteed after a barrel of corn was shelled and taken to the mill to grind. Cornbread was the weekend treat with candied yams and "that good ole clabber milk" buttermilk, still some of my dad's favorite foods. Some food was kept cold in the ice box, cooled by a seventy-five-pound block of ice in its bottom. Other perishables were put into the deep well for cooling. Big Momma did most of the cooking, but as the girls got older, they all took a part in preparing the family meals. Dad said his mother taught them all about love and being loving and kind to one another. She taught them to be obedient and to always listen and respect their elders.

He was called the "knee baby" boy because he was the second youngest of nineteen children from blended families. His next sibling, W. T., wouldn't be born for four years. His father Isaac (whom he called "Poppa") had fathered eight children before marrying the woman who would give birth to my Dad, Estella Sabbath (whom we called "Big Momma"). Large families were not unusual in the sharecropping culture of 1920s.

Most of the eleven children born to their union had nicknames, while others had just initials for their full names, except my Dad. His siblings were L.B., Dave (Dooley), Isaac (Bud), Eudora (Sis), Booker T. (Book), George (Dan), Soflunda (Coon), Ginnie Virginia (Ginnie

V.), LeRoy (Roy), and W.T. (renamed himself Zach). The four other siblings that my grandmother raised were Margaret (Mag), Bashna (Katie), Daisy (Lil Bit), and Roosevelt (Rock). The kids were taught that there were no half or whole siblings—they were all just sisters and brothers to each other. Dad's earliest memories are the sounds of his mother's voice sweetly singing to him "Yes Jesus loves me", and the smells of her homemade buttermilk biscuits and smoked bacon cooking in the wood-fired oven.

Their wood-framed house had four small bedrooms, a kitchen, and no indoor plumbing. It sat high off the ground on round-cut and stacked tree stumps. Poppa Isaac had built the house complete with a corrugated tin roof. Their mules and cows grazed and roamed on a pasture on the right side of the house. A family garden sat just past the low wooden fence that ran along the road before the house. "This down home life was good," Dad said, because it was filled with love and family all working together. The church was the center of their universe. Big Momma who also stored several hundred cans of different fruits, beans, and vegetables for the coming winters, sometimes sang in the fields, her voice joined by others working on their rows.

Both his mother and father sang in the church choir, and his older brothers had a gospel quartet. Most of his family sang in some way or another and quite often there was singing around him, so it came naturally for him.

Down home, the rooster's day-breaking crow would awaken them while chickens and an occasional dog roamed the sparse part-dirt and grass front yard. There were fruit trees, pear and peach, and a small woodshed where stored canned food was kept. Down the lane, there were a few scattered houses and a mulberry tree that my dad loved to climb, picking and tasting the dark, delicious, finger-staining berries.

Discipline was stiff. They got "whippins" not "spankins", most of the time with a leather razor strap, sometimes with a long green twig from a nearby tree. The wood-burning fireplace, built from a combination of wood, clay and Louisiana red dirt, was in the center of the house near the large pinewood dinner table. When it was lit, the smell of a warming crackling fire filled the entire house, with the gentle white smoke rising into the sky from its chimney.

Each night after a long, hard, and often hot day in the fields, Big Momma would heat water in a big kettle and mix that with regular well water for baths. Using about a seventeen-gallon, steel #3 tub, just long enough to squat and get yourself washed off, everyone bathed outside behind the kitchen. The water was changed after two or three kids used it, depending on how dirty it got. Baths were mandatory after chores on those long workdays. If it wasn't a heavy-duty workday, feet washing at a minimum was required.

The kids went to school six months out of the year. The other six were spent planting, plowing, sowing, reaping, hoeing, and drying or shelling peas and peanuts. As soon as they got home from school, they changed out of their homemade school clothes into work clothes so they could do their chores. Down home was a life of work and some play, sometimes just simple ball games; the boys would play with homemade cars, and the girls with homemade dolls. And baseball. Poppa Isaac would play baseball with them in the pasture, and though he stood 6'2" tall, nearly 250 pounds, Dad said he could run fast. There was also other games, dominos and Chinese checkers. Dad said that his father played and encouraged them in those games because he knew dominoes taught them how to count and strategize. Chinese checkers taught them how to count faster. Both were boys only games sometimes played at the dining table, but the girls were not allowed. They had jump rope, hopscotch, and other doll games. No whist or other card games because Poppa Isaac considered it gambling, which he strictly prohibited. He teasingly told the boys one day, "I worked hard to make a good name for myself in this Holly town. And if you mess up my name, I'll kill yah and make another one just like yah!"

Their parents were always teaching them the necessities of how to take care of themselves including how to slaughter and clean, cook, grow, harvest, wash and iron—everything it took to survive in that time. It was the only life they knew, except the eternal life they sang about when they would someday get to heaven.

There was a huge sense of community in his village. At the first cold snap, near early November, Dad said Poppa Isaac would kill and clean ten hogs with the help of many of the neighbors. In return, whoever came got a fair portion of the meat. For those who couldn't come for one reason or another, my grandfather would send cotton-sack wrapped packages of meat, hand-delivered by one of the sons, Booker T. My grandfather always shared with most everyone in the community, especially those less fortunate creating a sense of shared prosperity. They were strict, yet kind and giving parents who engendered an expectation of service. Hogs and cows were killed for meat two times a year for the family consumption. My dad was not a part of the killing because he said, "I just couldn't do it!" Hearing the screaming sounds of the animals dying at the slaughter was too much for his tender heart. The older boys would prepare the freshly slaughtered hogs and cows for their hickory smokehouse, where the meat would cure for several days. My dad would help his mother with indoor chores until that part was done. Poppa Isaac would also hunt rabbits, raccoons, possums, and quail with the older boys. He would skin them and Big Momma would clean and cook them up now and then, fried or smothered in gravy. They never knew a hungry day.

The sense of belonging, the work and purpose of close knit families working toward shared goals, the enveloping love of like-minded people who had a deep abiding faith, was a sweet time in my dad's life. These foundational years of his early childhood, when his family was independent and self-reliant, is what my dad recalls when he talks of down home—of having most of his siblings around and how they were interwoven into the hum and harmony of their work, home life, and faith. Dad says that they were treated like wealthy people, maybe because they were a strong family force in the community, but more likely because Poppa Isaac was revered not only for being an intelligent man of great faith, but one of deep compassion and generosity. He believed that if you were blessed by the good Lord to be prosperous, you should help others. And that's what he did, how he lived, and what he showed his children.

People used to ask my grandfather, "Ike, why you make those boys work so hard?" Poppa Isaac would say, "I gotta teach 'em how to work because I'm not gon' be with 'em always. Whatever job they get on, they'll be able to handle it, regardless of what it is." My dad says about his father, "He was one of the greatest men on earth. Yes, he was a fine man! He went to school for only three months and he made two grades in that time. He was so smart and could do math in his head. He helped people in the community, loved his family, and we all knew it. He taught me so many things about being a man and being respected. He was a leader. Everybody needs someone to look up to and for me, it was my daddy."

So a great dad, gave me one---and the story goes on.

"A whole village raised the chil'ren back then. If you got out of line, you could get a strap or a switch spankin' from one parent and you hoped they didn't tell your parents, because you could get another strappin' when you got home!" Dad recalls with a slight giggle. "There was a sense of everyone looking out for each other down home."

As the "knee baby" boy, my dad had a great viewpoint because he had so many older siblings he could learn from, and unconsciously observed how his parents managed their large vibrant family. He watched and absorbed how his father's hard work, love, and devotion to his family, his generosity of spirit, faith and great integrity showed great merit, and left a legacy in that sweet down home place in Holly. Dad brought those down home values and deep sense of family with him as he planted and watered the seeds of love, devotion, and generosity into the soil of our little family.

The original Stamper property located next to the Whitaker's eighty acres and almost identical to the Whitaker family's home

CHAPTER 3

Ain't Nothin' But Hair

We all called her Big Momma. Fair-skinned and green-eyed, Big Momma had a slim upper body and curvy full hips. We were always told that she was part American Indian, but we never knew which tribe. My father describes her this way: "She was an angel of the earth. Her hair come clean down to the top of her behind. Her green eyes were amazing. She was a beautiful woman."

Big Momma was a stunning Lena Horne-esque beauty, a hard-working mother, and a supportive mate to my grandfather. Big Momma seemed so light-skinned in contrast to Poppa Isaac's dark shade of Sudanese blue-black that most people in the community referred to her as "the white lady."

There was always so much work to be done on the farm, but among Big Momma's many household responsibilities, quilting was a priority. Along with trying to nurture her children and teach them in the ways of faith and family, she also had to keep them warm. She made several quilts annually for her family and other family members as they grew larger. When winter's wet cold would often freeze the north Louisiana ground solid for months of mornings at a time, their house could feel like an icebox.

Dad said that you could sometimes see the sky through the tin roof where it didn't connect at all the points. That was nice when it was warm out, and you could catch a twinkling star winking in the black night sky. "But when it rained," he said, "you'd have to move over so the drops didn't hit you." On cold winter nights, Big Momma would heat pressings irons in the fire, and then wrap them up in her homemade quilts and put them in the beds so the kids would have extra warmth through the night as the winter's wet wind whistled through the cracks of the slat walls. The children slept two or three together on shuck mattresses made from dried corn husk and straw stuffed with lint cotton; their body heat and those warming quilts got them through the wintery, sometimes wet nights.

Her quilting seemed like a hobby to her children because it was one of the few times she was still. In the noon day sun on a weekend, or in the cool of the early evening before the night dropped its starry blanketed sky, Big Momma would sit, sometimes stand and quilt. After his chores were done, young Green loved to hang around his mom while she quilted.

Big Momma kept her nearly waist length, soft, wavy medium-brown hair braided and tucked under a bonnet or tied up with a scarf so it stayed out of the way. Sitting between his mother and her sisters-in-law Rena and Lettie on one of those seemingly still afternoons, curious six-year-old Green asked his mother if he could brush her hair while she quilted. She obliged. That day stretched to many days and became a part of a pattern. Big Momma would sit around the wooden quilting slats sewing square-shaped cloths cut from colorful and patterned used flour sacks, sometimes leaning or reaching across the fabric and occasionally standing, but while he sat, he brushed her hair. Stitch by stitch with a needle and a thimbled thumb she sewed those squares into layers of warmth for her family—row by row, quilt by quilt. And there was young Green right beside her, as often as he could be, sometimes with a needle and thimble, and other times with a comb or brush, but learning either way.

One day, a lady passing by called out to my grandmother, "Stella! You lettin' that boy braid yo' hair?"

"Ain't nothin' but hair. Ain't gon' hurt him none, might learn somethin'," Big Momma replied without looking up from her quilting. My dad kept right on braiding, and he got pretty good at it.

Years later, with a wife and four growing children of his own – three of them daughters – my dad was still braiding hair. In the morning routine of our family, there was breakfast to make, lunches to pack, beds to make, homework to gather, and hair to comb before getting the four of us out the door. My dad would sit, brush and braid one daughter's hair, while Ola Mae, did another.

My elementary school teacher asked me once with slight amusement upon seeing my neat but a slightly imperfect hair, "Who combed your hair?"

"Daddy did!" I replied with great enthusiasm.

When I was growing up, we visited my grandmother nearly every Sunday after church. If it was warm out, sometimes she would quilt outside. And, just as my dad did, she would sit, take off her bonnet or scarf and let me brush and braid her hair.

My dad says this taught him a lesson in just letting a child be. It didn't make him any less a boy and perhaps helped him become more of a man in the learning. I see it as freedom from gender-scripted behavior. Combing hair is just that. Life is full of useful tools and skills of all sorts; my grandmother had taught my father a lovely lesson that day.

Estella and Isaac Whitaker

CHAPTER 4

Black Gold

Poppa Isaac had purchased outright the eighty-acre tract of land in the early part of the twentieth century on which my father and his siblings lived on and were born and raised. They were farmers growing and selling their own cotton, peas, and vegetables. He earned extra money occasionally by building up new roads in the surrounding area, and the children could earn and extra 35 cents per day hoeing grass for the Stamper family who lived on the next farm down the road when they were caught up working on their own farm. In 1930, when my dad was four years old, oil was discovered on their land in Holly, a rural town with an estimated population of nearly 400. The oil was a big deal all around, but for my dad, his most exciting memory of that time was the day his Poppa Isaac drove a new car into their dusty yard one sunny afternoon when he was four years old.

Young Green, wearing his homemade overalls, was taken by the hand and led to their family's brand new maroon Buick car with silver disc wheels. He had never seen anything so beautiful or shiny. He could see the reflection of his face looking back at him, wide-eyed and open-mouthed, in the mirror-like wheels. Several family members ran out when they heard the humid Louisiana air filled with "oohs" and "aahs" from those gathered around to see and smell the car's gleaming newness in the afternoon sun.

Big Momma came out, wiping her wet hands on her apron, to join the inspection and admiration. Young Green could hardly contain his excitement. The car could hold six adults and perhaps several Whitaker children squeezed in its two rows of vinyl black bench seats. There were large roll-down windows, two headlights at the end of the long-nosed hood, silver chrome stripes above the front wheels, and a storage compartment behind the backseat. Unlike Poppa Isaac's small used dull Whippet 6, you could even see your face reflected in the paint.

During that time, it was quite exceptional for anyone, especially a black man, to own a car. America had plunged into the Great Depression, and though a few families had cars, many in the rural areas were still using mules, horses, and buggies for work and transportation over the dusty trampled grass roads to get to town or church. The oil well discovered on their property, the biggest well reservoir ever found in Holly, enabled Poppa Isaac to afford the new car.

As the exploratory well drilled deeper and deeper, day by day, the pumping rig became a familiar part of the family's property and the children played around its imposing archaic form, but knew not to climb the wooden triangular support structure.

Poppa Isaac had a feeling that oil was in abundance when one day a man, probably a rig manager, came to their house to say it was time to "pull the cap." Dad remembers how the crude oil, the black gold, gushed up and ran like black snakes, slithering and twisting over the grassy earth, some of it flying into the air. The rhythmic strokes of the pump brought oil up from the deep underground reservoirs uninterruptedly for several years. Occasionally, official-looking white men would come and offer as much as $75,000 for the rights or to buy the rig. That would have been like getting a million dollars back then. Poppa Isaac figured if they wanted that much money, it had to be worth much more. So, he didn't sell. After six years or so, some of those people went across the road and drilled horizontally until they tapped into the well of oil on the Whitaker property.

I learned that saltwater and brine were used in the old drilling process in the 1930s. When the Whitaker well was tapped, that meant the oil was probably moved to another well. Instead of oil coming up out of the drill hole, saltwater seeped up and into the soil. The land became untenable because "saltwater spills can make the soil and crops infertile for many years," my dad said. No longer able to produce crops on the land which they lived, they could not stay and survive there. The well was eventually capped. It wasn't uncommon for illicit drillers to tap into neighboring reservoirs, but it was common knowledge that a black man couldn't fight the stealing of his oil on his land or take legal action; it simply wasn't done. Dad was 10 years old when the Whitaker's beloved eighty acres was sold and the family was forced to move. The whole family cried for two weeks when knew they had to leave their loving home. They were very sad but they were also angry. There was no one to fight the battle of trying to keep their land and they were forced to accept this bitter loss. This is the real black gold black men weren't allowed to keep-- their land. And just like that, they went from landowners to sharecroppers, a family who worked and shared land on a plantation.

With some of the money Poppa Isaac made and saved from their crops and what the oil production yielded, he purchased 120 acres of mostly forested land for the family, and moved to live on a share-cropper farm in Gayle, up the road about twelve miles. Dad refers to it as the "house down by the river." Even with the loss of the oil and the family land, what kept them going was their love for one another; their home was still full of love and a had sense of well-being. For a time, it had been Camelot.

They had lived in that beautiful rural bubble in that sweet place in Holly, while the rest of Louisiana and the nation were gripped in dealing with recovery from the Great Depression, targeted discrim-ination, economic strife, and bigoted violence. For whatever blessed reasons, these farmers and churchgoers seemed shielded from some of that ugliness, cocooned in that farming village for a time. Dad remembered that his life was always filled with the love, simple joys, and protection of his family. It was a time he always cherished.

CHAPTER 5
Gimme That Old Time Religion

———◆———

Most of the rituals and traditions of the southern Baptist churches date back a couple centuries before my dad was born. Many of the customs started when slaves adopted Christianity and carried that forth to the cotton fields of my father's farming and sharecropping days, and through today in the sometimes woeful minor tones in some of the music.

My dad's home church growing up was Mount Moriah Baptist, not far from their home in Holly. When he was a boy, church services were held only once a month. There was a separate building next to the church for the children to go to Sunday school, and in the winter months, they'd have to walk down to the woods, chop some pine wood, and bring it back to make a fire there. Once the fire was started, the boys had to stand back and let the girls get warmed first, even though they were just as cold. "Ladies first we were taught," Dad said. And they did what they were told by their elders which planted the seeds of chivalry he carried throughout his adult life.

The congregants were a community coming to worship. Uncles, cousins, neighbors, and everyone else were farmers, so they had a shared experience and lived a parallel existence. The preaching was revival-style theatrical: the call-and-response hymns, the sacred beautiful music, and "the people was so lovely and kind to each other," Dad said. Among the church's deacons were Poppa Isaac and his brother Ake Whitaker, Noba Bates and a gentleman Dad remembers as Deacon Gus. These were the names of men that helped lead the service and set the standards for manners and church etiquette that my father looked up to. Dad said his parents didn't just "go to church", they brought all the family with them to experience worship service in that crowded, spirited, country church.

In turn, he and Mother brought us all to church every Sunday. I too was born into a church life and it was all consuming, full of love of community, and Christ. It was a Monday through Sunday thing between choir practices and bible study. The church was also the center for gathering and social connections outside of family. At the church our family attended, the services always began with what we called devotions, a call-and-response hymn called the "Old One-Hundreds" usually led by a deacon. In response, the congregation would follow his call with the echoing of the song in harmony, always in a minor key, which lent melancholy to it.

"I love the Lord, he heard my cry!" one of the deacons would sing in a loud, strong, assured tone. *"Iiiiiii, I love the Lorrrd, he heard myyy cryyy"*, the church echoed back.

"Annnnnnnnnd piiiitied ehhhhhhh vrrrryyy groannn...", the congregation sang back in a choir-like response like the dull roar of a coming tide. This was the beginning of the worship service.

The swell of voices would rattle the windows and expand with a sound that rose up like the rush of a mighty river overflowing its banks and seeping into the thirsty grassy earth. *"Lonnnnng as I live while trouble rise!"* the deacon would sing out, the congregation echoing back in the sing-song manner, then *"I'll haaaaasten to His throne!"* And as they sang back to him the church's voices would be punctuated with *"Yes Lord! and Thank ya Jesus!"*

The harmonic waves gathered in the damp air inside the old wooden church. You could feel them in the planks. The sound leaked out of its walls and was carried away over the surrounding fields. This communal melding music felt tribal and unfiltered, a pool of harmonic wailing both woeful and joyful, primitive and new. Often punctuated with claps and "amens", in that atmosphere the music seeped into each person and became a physical expression of praise. After the song, one of the Deacons would kneel and pray an old-school, out-loud prayer in a sing-song manner, with a calm and sincere voice saying, "Father God, I come humbly before you today, head bowed and body bent." All eyes were closed across the church, babies rocked by their mothers momentarily quieted as he prayed without a microphone. "Lord, I wanna thank you for waking me up this morning and starting me on my way," he continued.

A lady in the church whisper-shouted, "Yessuh Lord!" as the deacon continued. "That I was closed in my right mind, and the bed I laid on was not my cooling board; the kiver I covered with, not my winding sheave."

The congregation hummed while voices rose and fell into some intrinsic known harmonies. People were rocking side to side or back and forth as the prayer began lighting the fire of worship to come. They listened as one and openly agreed with shout-outs to his praying. The deacon's voice moved up a pitch to another gear: "Thank ya Lord, that you kept me when I didn't know how to keep myself. Thank ya that you never left me." The congregation talked back in low voices as he prayed, egging him on "My Lord today!", and "Say that!" The deacon's voice took on a song-like cadence, elongating some words, going deeper with his song-type prayer voice rising and falling with a sacred fervor, both eyes closed, head bowed on a bended knee... "Thank ya for everyday that You brought me out. Thank ya for the food on my table and a roof over my head!"

"THANK YA LORD!" another deacon shouted out.

The praying deacon's voice began to swell louder. "Lorrrddd, I ask you...to have mercy on us." He sang the words. "Stop by the church, Lord, and touch those who are sick in their bodies. Stop by and touch your people today. Stop by Lord and have your way!" He paused for a moment to let the congregation catch up and catch its breath. "Bless us now Lord and keep us in your love." A pause and then, "And then my Father, when my tiiime is done down here, when it's aaawlll over Lord. "Ovah Lord! Ovah Lord!" echo chanted the congregants.

The revenant words echoed all over the church from the faithful worshippers. Many closed-eyed congregants wiped away streaming tears, others waved their hands in the air in spiritual surrender. The deacon then brought his prayer to an end, his voice back down to the monotone delivery he'd begun with, "When I can't study war no mo'..."

Likewise, the congregants softened their voices to whispers while the mothers fanned their babies with cardboard fans and pressed hard candy into the hands of toddlers to keep them quiet and still in the rising humid air. The body heat rose as the prayer reverberated within the slat walls, the pew planks, and floorboards of the church. People said separately and together, "Yes SUH!" and "Glory Today!"

The deacon brought his tone down more. "I wanna hear you say Servant of God, GOOD and faithful servant. Well done! Come take yo' rest." He paused to bring the prayer to a close: "And we give you ALL the praise and glory!! Amen!"

"AMEN!" the congregation repeated.

The spirit of praise had been ignited like low fire under a simmering pot, the praise brought to low boil, which set the tone for the worship service to follow. The choir sang a song and then the service was underway. That was how our church services began each Sunday.

We attended the same Baptist church my dad had joined when he was eighteen. Mary Evergreen Baptist Church was a white wood-framed building that stood on cinder block pillars. It had a worn white wooden steeple atop its center with an old tarnished brass bell that was only rung by the elder statesman of the church, Deacon Oscar Johnson, when there was a funeral procession.

The church stood off the two-lane asphalt Highway 175 in Frierson, and down a tire-tracked dirt lane that was marked only by an almost hidden low flag. It was set back in a grassy clearing on land that also belonged to the Frierson family, who my father and his siblings had picked cotton for many years. The church was a twenty-minute drive from our home in the community of Cedar Grove.

Tall trees surrounded the church on two sides, giving it a pristine green isolation that made its white color especially bright in contrast against the backdrop. When it rained, which it did often, that narrow dirt road became a long muddy pit, making it hard for people to get to the church without getting their cars stuck. Some days, we'd have to park off the side of the highway and walk, muddying up our

Sunday shoes. Still, the people packed in every Sunday, rain or shine, muddied shoes and all. The singing and the way they worshipped and praised God was hypnotic and deeply inspired, rolling out of the plantation fields into a praise of salvation and the hope of eternal life.

After the devotion of the Old One-Hundred Hymn and the prayer, the church secretary gave a welcome address to any new or returning visitors, followed by the reading of church announcements for upcoming meetings and other general information. A roll call of those members who were sick and shut in their homes or hospital followed and melded into an altar call, where the congregation gathered at the center altar table to pray closer together while the choir sang softly as the underscore.

There were two collection plates, one for a "penny offering" along with a regular one. Congregants often put coins instead of dollars in that collection plate and the sum went to helping people who were sick and not able to attend, so we were told. Most put in whatever they were able. Our parents gave us nickels and later quarters that we tucked in our small purses to place in the offering plates. The congregation stood and moved by row as each passed by the center altar, where they placed their monetary offerings in the two collection plates flanked by deacons. The choir sang an upbeat song like, "Have you got good religion? Certainly Lord!", "Jesus lifted me", or "Holding on to My Faith." Some women would hand off their little babies to other mothers during the offering as the church was burgeoning with young members and growing families. I loved seeing the wriggling brown babies handed over as a symbol of trust and love all over the church.

For me, it was also a time to see all the fanciful colorful dresses the ladies of the church wore. Whether fitted and flared or belted and snug, each looked beautiful to me. Some of the women wore rouge and lipstick and maybe a little powder. Their hair was pressed and curled under varying sized and colored hats that coordinated with their dresses. Some wore gloves, while all wore slips, bras, girdles, and stockings with garters underneath. Women wore low-heeled fancy shoes, while most children wore patent leather church shoes, the girls with fold-down socks, some with lace along with their Sunday clothes. Pants or pant suits were never worn by ladies; it was forbidden at that time in the Baptist tradition. When the last of the offering was taken, a prayer of thanks followed. The choir downshifted to a more ballad-like gospel song, such as "You Can't Beat God's Giving, No Matter How You Try."

The deacons usually dressed in dark colors on communion Sundays, the first Sunday of the month. A tradition was about the consecrated remembrance of the crucifixion of Christ; the sharing of broken saltine crackers (representing His broken body), and grape juice in small individual glass communion cups (representing the blood He shed) served for all the members. The choir sang underneath while we again proceeded around the altar and received our communion, taking a piece of cracker, then drinking the hand-poured juice from several small cups half-full and placing it back. It was understood that if you were not baptized, you could not partake. On other Sundays, the men could dress with varied colored suits, shirts and skinny ties. Since most of the men worked farm or blue collar jobs, the opportunity to dress up away from the sweat stained or rote uniforms of their weekly work was welcomed. The men too enjoyed putting on their "Sunday best" suits and shoes and shirts with ties to match. If their outfits were put together well, others would comment that they were "cleaner than the board of health!"

On those non-communion Sundays, after the offering, the choir would sing an "A and B selection" (two songs) leading into the pastor's sermon. Slowly rising to stand behind a wooden podium centered in the pulpit, wearing a traditional black calf-length clergy robe with bulbous sleeves and wide black velvet stripes down its front, the Pastor began his sermon with a scripture reading. Other ministers, whether visiting or being mentored, sat on either side in tall-backed wooden chairs with small cushioned seats. They would stand along with deacons and the church elders while the scripture was being read. Next, the Pastor stated the sermon title or topic, which he would repeat with the congregation to prepare themselves for the lesson and the full gospel preaching to come. He began slowly, his words sure, direct, and elongated for punctuation and definition. He'd say a phrase, and if the response was slow, he'd add, "Oh, I wish I had a witness today!" This would elicit some laughs in agreement. The church would respond, "Say it Preacher!" and "Come on preacha, Preach!" and "Amen Lord!" Some of the church ladies started to fan themselves as the body heat in the building started to rise. He expounded and roused the people with the pitch and inflection of his voice as the church talked back in agreement and acknowledgement.

My dad said that, "'Amen' to a preacher was like 'sick'em' to a dog!" The more the congregation engaged and responded, the stronger the tone of his voice became, his whole body engaged in the sermon. He used rhythm and phrasing like a good singer who knew where to put the emphasis, where to hold a note and how to release. It was musical, magical, and mighty powerful. He'd say a sentence in his sermon, and if he didn't get a response, he'd add, "I don't think you heard me!" and repeat the sentence again which would get everyone's attention.

This whooping style of preaching sometimes had a Shakespearean quality, the ability to present ideas with dramatic phrasing. When he was hitting the right chords about the goodness or wrath of God, or in retelling a story of Jesus's life, throwing in a modern comparison to the parables or the miracles, the congregation would joyfully talk back to him in the ebb and flow of his sermon. "And then God said stretch out the rod in your hand...What's your rod?!" or "Jesus took those two fish and five loaves of bread..." the preacher would say excitedly, and someone would yell out, "Tell it!" or "Preach the gospel!" or "OOOH God Today!"

As the sermon progressed, his tone and fervor grew along with the congregation. It was as if he conducted the orchestra of the church; his vocal intonations created the tempo, rhythm and volume as he rose to the apex of the music in his text. He took his time getting to the climax of his topic. "And when she looked and saw she was healed...", he said, pausing and getting full of the holy spirit shaking his head... "Oh My God...Did you know that God can heal you?"

The members would talk back in elevated tones, "Yes He Will!"

"Sho nuff!"

The Pastor continued, "When the doctors have done all they can do, Man's end is God's beginning! GOD is in the healing business today!"

The church was on fire now and somebody or another was filled with the holy spirit — or as they called it, the "Holy Ghost" — or they "got happy" and jumped to their feet, shouts accented with foot-stomping, arms raised up in praise and faces wet with rejoicing tears. Ushers run over to fan and soothe one, then another. In a punctuated, slow deliberate black Southern cadence with pauses and room for responses, he reached the climax of his sermon, telling of the sacrifice of Christ dying on Calvary Hill. "He paid it all! Your sins! My sins! He died for the SINS of the world!" "Do you know that GOD is able to make a way out of no way?!" He is practically singing like a soul singer as the piano underscored him. "When you don't know which way to turn, he'll make a way!"

Then the preacher made a vowel sound like a car trying to start, "Iiiiii'mmm a witness today!" — and abruptly sat down.

The drama of this abrupt ending only added to the ripened exhilaration, the deacons standing with holy ghost cheering, and the whole church clapping, many on their feet, their hands up in praise, shouting, "Yes He can! MY Lord!" The church was whipped up into a frenzy, the choir adding the final touches with a rousing choir song that carried everybody over the top with their praise. The Holy Ghost would whip around that church with folks shouting, fainting, running, more shouting, dancing, and praising all over the place.

Joy, pain, tears, rejoicing all blended into these surreal Holy Spirit moments that came Sunday after Sunday. Some said it was like "fire shut up in my bones" when the Holy Spirit moved within them, and there was a freedom in the wails and shouts that filled the church.

The pastor would stand again once the choir was almost done. "Won't you come today...Accept Christ as your personal Savior." Piano music played gently underneath his words of invitation. The church service always ended with the pastor asking if there was someone who wanted to join. It was called opening the doors of the church. They could come by way of a "letter", if they wanted to leave another church to join ours, by "Christian experience", if that person didn't have a church home but had been baptized, or if just joining the church for the first time, they were required to be baptized by submergence in water. The deacons would stand with their arms extended towards the congregation while he made the invitation; my dad was one of them. If someone walked forward, he or she was greeted with great praise, hand claps, amens and "Hallelujah!" from the entire congregation.

My dad was very active in the church. He was the Deacon's chairman for many years, as well as President of the choir. He was a lead part of these old-time religious services I grew to know and love. He would sometimes sing a solo with the choir backing, and the people would shout and shout. He helped with everything from the devotion, to the offering and tallying up the intake, singing in the choir and the invitation to join the church, as did all the deacons.

I always felt such pride watching my daddy there. I saw him doing it. I saw him helping. I saw his love of the church and being a leader in it. I witnessed him be an active, willing, devoted member who loved God. His faith spilled onto us. He was just as devoted to our family. He and Mother shared a vision; that their children would grow up knowing the word of God, with solid church and family values, using the Bible teachings as a compass for all lives. They didn't force it on us, but used their example of kindness and the way they lived to help teach us the lessons we needed to learn.

From a young girl's perspective, all the people in the church were the same, each other's extended family. There were no high or low people, no celebrities, no lawyers or doctors, just everyday working-class people worshipping together. From the pastor to the ushers, there seemed to be a real care and concern for the life of the church and its members; the pastor knew every name and every family. As an adult, I now understand that the church was a place of safety, realignment and release for those congregants. They were free there where they couldn't be in other parts of their lives. I know that churches like any entity or family, can have drama and secrets, but growing up, I was not aware of it except for some nasty boys who used to taunt me and my sister by hitting us or pulling our ponytails and running, or putting frogs in the back of the camper when we rode to and from choir rehearsals. Mommy said those playful hits were love pats and that it meant they liked us, but I didn't like them or feel very loving or Christian toward them.

Some of the older members of the church had been sharecroppers and some still were farmers; others had moved on to blue collar factory jobs up in the city, or whatever solid work they could get, teacher, bus drivers, librarians. This was a working-class church full of hard-working black folk who came together each Sunday to worship in this old-time way, the only way they knew and the way they had learned. We all belonged, we each felt blessed and lifted. Sometimes it felt otherworldly, but I was always moved by the music, the way it sat in my chest and imprinted my heart, its meanings and tradition a treasured part of my upbringing. It sings in my soul to this day. The old song would say, "Gimme that old time religion, it's good enough for me!"

I couldn't agree more.

CHAPTER 6

Take The Water!

For two weeks at the end of July, the church held its annual revival services. Reminiscent of the old tent revivals (without the acts of healing and the tent), it consisted of two weeks of evening church services where the congregation worshipped and prayed for saving sinners' souls. At our home, our parents had us kneel and pray three times daily during those weeks.

On these warm summer nights, the ladies wore cool cotton dresses, while the men were dressed in pants, skinny ties, and light-weight shirts. People filled every pew. Everyone's skin was shiny from the thick moist heat inside the un-air-conditioned church. With fans fanning and heels clicking on the wood-planked floors, all joined in singing the congregation and choir songs with bottoms seated on plain wooden pews, hungry for the communion of these yearly "come-to-Jesus" nights. They hung on every word the pastor spoke and helped him along by talking back, saying loudly, "Say that, Preach-er!" or "OOHHHH, Jesus!" and "YES, Lord!"

It was a sacred praise-filled time in the community village, praying for souls both new and old to join the church. Witnessing this as a little girl, I felt like I was watching a growing tide of praise each night. To join the church and become a member, you had to sit on the "mourner's bench" (we called it the "moaning bench" because that's how they pronounced it). The mourner's bench was the front pew of the church, usually reserved for the deacons and deaconesses on regular Sunday mornings. When their conviction spoke or the Holy Spirit moved them, they would come forth and confess their belief that Jesus would save their soul. Since the mission of the Baptist faith is to save lost souls, this confession was the pinnacle of that mission.

After devotions, choir songs, offering collections and an impas-sioned sermon for that evening, the pastor and deacons would face the congregation. Deacons, including my dad, extended white-gloved hands to invite those on the mourner's bench to come sit in one of the chairs facing out toward the congregation, while the choir or a soloist sang in the background. This extension also happened every Sunday after the preacher's sermon, which was called "opening the doors of the church." But during revival, it was an invitation to begin the faith walk of accepting Jesus as your savior and to have your soul saved. My dad was one of those deacons with his hand extended.

If you were in those front seats, you had to decide when the time was right for you, based on when you felt moved to do so, or by the Holy Spirit moving through you. I didn't understand fully what that was or felt like back then, but people talked about it. When they felt the Holy Spirit, there would be shouting and running, jumping and sometimes quiet crying. The expression of the spirit brought a range of big emotions that seemed at times wild, but also somehow sweet and bewildering. I could also feel the release and joy in it, too. This was a place where you could shout and cry and let go of whatever was pent up inside, then rejoice.

When my dad was a boy, revival weeks began in early August. It was a sacred time in the community as they prayed for the young and old, and themselves if they were "unsaved."

My dad had been a somewhat shy boy who was remarkably close to his mother. Her words meant everything to him. Big Momma said that for a person to "confess Christ," they had to have experienced something supernatural. She told this to all her children, because she wanted to be sure they had experienced a unique and singular sign from God. She would often ask them, "Has the Lord done anything for ya?"

When he was about twelve, Dad and his closest brother, LeRoy, eleven months older and whom we called Roy, were hanging around an oak tree so large that they could stand on either side and not see each other. Suddenly, out of a clear blue sky, the air filled with the most angelic voices singing a song neither of them knew, but was more beautiful than either had ever heard.

My dad called out, "Roy! Did you hear that?"

"Yeah!" said Roy. "It's like a choir somewhere up there. Can you see anything?"

They both looked up, gazing through the leafed branches, and squinted into the sun to try to find the source of the sound.

"Sho is pretty. Prettiest I ever heard," said Roy.

Both boys looked up and around for where this sound could be coming from. They saw nothing but the branches and the blue sky above. Then they realized they were hearing and experiencing something supernatural, something angelic and holy, and they both knew it. They also knew they could not tell Big Momma of this shared supernatural experience because it would seem made up. But Dad knew that it was time for him to take to the mourner's bench. With this angelic voice experience, he felt he was ready to join the church.

My dad said he always felt a deep spiritual connection with the Almighty, even at a young age, and was repeatedly told he was wise beyond his years. He truly believed that God would do something supernatural in his life. He sat on that "moaning" bench for two weeks, and each night he prayed for God to give him a special sign, asking, "Lord if you want me to confess, then don't let me be able to stand up." Each night, after the preacher preached and the choir chorused and the deacons stood with hands reaching out while the congregation sang, my dad was able to stand tall and sing along with the congregational song.

On the last night of the revival, when the deacons extended their white-gloved hands, he tried to stand but couldn't. When he shared this story with me, he said, "I…I kept trying and trying, but I couldn't."

As he recalled this, he paused and burst into tears. With a choked voice, he said, "I was trying to stand up and look like some-thin' had a holt to my knees! I kept trying to stand and then …It's hard to talk about it, even now. But when I come to, I was in my momma's arms with tears streaming down her face, and she was say-ing, 'It's okay baby, it's all right!'"

Dad knew the Holy Spirit had done something mighty powerful in his young life and body that night, and that experience shaped his spiritual journey. This was how it happened for him eighty-two years ago and he has been a church-going God-filled man since.

And so, these traditions were passed down and carried on when I was a young girl. At our church, after the second week of revival, all those who had left the mourner's bench and taken a chair facing the congregation were candidates for baptism on the first Sunday in August, the biggest church day of the year. Congregants would cook all day Saturday in anticipation of this very special Sunday. Everyone dressed in their finest, with the congregation's women in wide colorful hats and color-coordinated purses and shoes. They were colorful and as cool as they could be in August air so hot that it felt like walking inside an oven. There were some small electric fans around the church to help move the stifling heat, but most people held paper fans with pictures of famous black people or advertisements from local funeral homes.

The wide slow-moving creek that ran behind the church had a muddy bottom that colored the water brown. It always looked dirty to me. The grassy banks of the creek sloped up to the mowed grass of the church grounds. On Baptizing Sunday, people came to church the same time as regular Sunday service, but instead of going into the sanctuary, the congregation gathered at the creek's grassy wide edge. Men, women and children lined up, waiting for the procession of those to be baptized.

The deacons in our Baptist church were a group chosen for their devout attributes, assisting the pastor and reaching out to the community. The deaconesses served a similar but lower position in the church hierarchy. She was usually the wife of a deacon and a selected lady of the church with similar attributes. The definition of deacon means "to serve or minister." One of these men, dressed casually with a white cotton sheath covering, was chosen to walk waist deep into the water and leave a pole there to mark where it was safe to walk. Most black people did not know how to swim, and this was an important role to play; it was the safety check for both the pastor and the baptized. It was a quiet and reverent time when the wading of the water began.

That was followed by the pastor being escorted down the slanted grassy slope, deacons flanking him on either side, into the water where the pole stood. This creek could have been a brown fishing hole on other days, but on Baptizing Sunday, it became sacred holy cleansing water.

Next, the baptized ones would be escorted out by the deaconesses to the grassy slope, where they would wait for their turn to be submerged. They lined up dressed barefoot and dressed in casual clothes and white sheaths, with a white covering for girls' heads. As we watched, the pastor would raise his hand high, holding a white towel, and say, "Do you believe that Jesus is the son of God?"

"I do!" was the reply.

"Do you believe that He died for our sins?"

"I do believe!"

Finally, he would say, "In Obedience to God's commandments and upon the profession of your faith, I baptize you in the name of the Father, The Son, and The Holy Spirit!" The pastor would cover their face with the towel (sometimes, the baptizees would pinch their own noses) and then they would be dipped backward, completely submerged in the water. This ceremony was repeated until everyone had been baptized. Some of the church ladies would begin to shout, "TAKE THE WATER!" "TAKE THE WATER!" in jubilation as the person was being baptized. When the baptized were raised out of water—some with arms raised in praise, others shouting, still others shedding quiet tears—they were met with claps and praise, wailing cries, and rejoicing, with exuberant "Hallelujah!" in celebration of their renewal.

At Mount Moriah church, where my dad was baptized, as many as one hundred people, young and old, would be submerged on their special day. It was a family church, where cousins and uncles and neighbors worshipped together. Thirty-four people were baptized on the day of my father's baptism in the neighborhood's Jewitt fish pond across the road. Church members had gathered around its pond's edge to witness, praise, and celebrate. Someone yelled, "Wait, Wait! We got Ike's boys here that need to get baptized!" They arrived late that Sunday, but upon seeing them, the pastor, Reverend Kelly Keys waded back into the pond to baptize Green and his brother LeRoy.

Once the newly baptized, pastor, and deacons dried and re-dressed, a church service followed, the deaconesses dressed in white with hats and gloves, and the deacons in black suits with white shirts. The entire service was a celebration of that annual day of baptism. It was a time of freedom in worship that was organic, raw, real, and full of hope that the love of Jesus could bring change and peace and a forgiveness of sins; a celebration of eternal life. The new church members sat attentively through the impassioned sermon, reciting some special Baptist creed along with the congregation, each given their own Bible. At nearly two o'clock in the afternoon, the service was finished and a group of tired, praised-out, hungry church-goers left the church, in need of nourishment.

And then a regal country feast began.

Church members brought food packed in the trunks of their cars. Hats and jackets came off and ties were loosened. Some of the women pulled aprons from their cars to protect their Sunday clothes. Some mothers stopped to bottle or breast-feed their young babies. Children ran uninhibited around the grassy parking lot, giggling, playing chase, in anticipation of the good eats. The trunks all sprang open one by one to reveal homemade foods covered in cloth. It was all homemade goodness: potato salad, fried and grilled and barbequed chicken, fish, cakes and pies. Someone always had some cold pop including Coca-Colas in those thick green-tinted glass bottles, Nehi strawberry or grape pop, water out of a jug, and usually homemade lemonade.

Dad said that each year, Poppa Isaac would kill a cow and a hog a few weeks ahead of their revival week. My grandmother would cook up all the cured meats, and make cakes and pies in her wood burning oven. They would pack all those homemade good foods into a big trunk and load it into a wagon hitched to a mule. Afterwards, people would come with their plates and eat and eat and eat. Everyone want-ed some of my grandmother's delicious foods and it seems a good country feast was always part of the big baptizing Sundays.

Ms. B. Hawkins, a stout, dark-skinned lady at our church, made the best lemon pound cake, and Aunt Ginnie V. made the best biscuits and fried chicken. Deacon Jamison made the best barbeque chicken and hot links, and Wyoming Demery had the tastiest coconut cake. Aunt Margaret's egg pie and jelly cake were famous, and my mother made a delicious pound cake and skillet cream corn. Another lady made a hoe cake (a large homemade biscuit made in a cast iron skillet) and everyone could make okra, rice, and great pot of collard or mustard greens with ham hocks. Somebody had chitlins, too, which I avoided. We'd go from car to car with a fork and paper plate, piling just enough of the delicious food upon it, then we would sit on the church steps or in a car seat with an opened door, and feast till we popped then usually fell asleep on the ride home, full of church and good food. Fresh and homemade, it was some of the best foods I've eaten complimented by the fellowship I witnessed of what felt like true brotherhood and a community of family.

When it was my time to sit on the mourner's bench, my parents talked with me about making this decision. There was never any pressure, but I was ready at the ripe age of six. I was old for my years I've been told, and when I walked to the front and spoke my confession, the church shouted all over. The day I was baptized was the first day I remember seeing my daddy cry. He was so proud of the commitment I was making; the whole church was. They hugged me and told me so. The men and women of my church, Deacons Joe Pierre, Cleotis Sutton, James Franklin, Calvin Thomas, my dad, Isaac Whitaker (my Uncle Bud), Eddie Flemming; and the Deaconesses Rosemary Pierre, Sally Flemming, my mom Ola Mae Whitaker, Isabella Robinson, Henrietta Thomas, and Atlina Johns, surrounded and supported all the baptized. I didn't have to go into that muddy creek, though. By then, they had installed an indoor baptizing pool, which was a square three-foot-deep tub, large enough for the pastor and one other to stand in waist-deep water. In the back of my mind, I knew I did not want to be dipped in that froggy muddy water of the creek.

I "took the water" as did my daddy, my mother, and all my siblings; we were all baptized. We learned how to walk in the Baptist tradition of the Christian faith in that sweet rural north Louisiana church filled with beautiful music, bountiful praise, the traditions of salvation and the cleansing power of the water through baptism.

These memories sit with me because it was a part of my rearing and what I saw in my church. It was old-fashioned, otherworldly, supernatural, and maybe out of step with the quieter services of other religious traditions. But in that little white wooden church down a dirt lane, the shouting, praying, Holy Ghost time was real, sacred, heartfelt, and infectious. I loved that it showed me the religious tradition of a people that has mostly been lost, or changed. The memories of that kind of worship, celebration, and communal trunk feasts are still so vivid in my mind; the pictures play like a beautiful beloved movie in my head.

I have tremendous appreciation for my parents raising us with these rich customs and celebratory experiences. It makes me feel warm and grateful for having witnessed and participated in it.

CHAPTER 7

Christmas, Plantation Style

Christmas has always been one of my favorite holidays because of how magical our parents made it for us. It was also their anniversary day, so there were extra special treats for our mother that Dad always surprised her with, like a pearl necklace, a fox fur wrap, and a silver tea service set for their 25th.

In the weeks before the holiday, Dad would hang colorful big-bulb Christmas lights around the front of our home. Then we'd get the large worn white cardboard box from the attic (a pull-down ladder from the ceiling in the hall unfolded and the large box lived up there most of the year), which contained our beloved silver tinsel tree. The tree was made of two three-foot silver rods, with holes up and down its shafts, that we connected end-to-end. Each metal branch with silver tinsel would fit into one of the holes, ultimately creating a perfectly shaped Christmas tree. At night, we would plug in a low-angled hot white lamp to shine onto a round rotating plastic wheel with pie-shaped slices of green, yellow, and red, changing the tree's color. The light reflected upon the silver tinsel tree as it peeked through the curtains of the large picture framed front window. It felt magical.

Christmas morning brought goodies wrapped in brightly colored paper and bows beneath the tree. The Santa gifts were hidden in different places around the living room/dining room where the upright piano also lived. We'd get some clothes and a special doll or toy, modest by today's standards, but we were thrilled that Santa had come. Sometimes before the big morning, my sister and I would shake one of the brightly colored boxes with our name on it to see if we could figure out the gift inside.

At our local Sears Roebuck department store, where Dad worked part-time for a few years, we would tell our Christmas wishes to a joyful jolly white Santa—complete with a long white beard, red and white velvet suit, and black belted at the waist. Seeing Santa there felt as though jolly Saint Nick from the storybooks had come to life from the North Pole, just to visit us, ever so gentle and plausible and real. It didn't occur to us or seem strange, having a black family and living in a black neighborhood that Santa was a white guy; it's how he was painted in all the pictures and books.

However, our ritual was a stark contrast to my father's plantation-style Christmas experience. There were no lights hung or brightly wrapped gifts. Instead, a few nights before Christmas, there would be a knock at the door after the children heard something on the roof. Poppa Isaac would see who was knocking, and when the door opened, a painted black- or red-faced black Santa stood there, dressed in red and white with a big fat belted belly.

The eleven children were frightened beyond words at this gruesome-looking, gruff-voiced man who threatened to "git" them if they had not been good. So frightening was he for the young children that some would run and hide under the beds or the table. Poppa Isaac would give Santa a big punch in that fat belly and away he'd run, while the children cowered in a corner of the house, watching as their father yelled after him, "Git on way from my chillen! Git outta here and don't come back!" Poppa Isaac was a hero for saving them, and they felt safe and saved. A day or so later, he'd instruct the children to put their saved shoe boxes on the floor near the fireplace to see if Santa would leave something for them. Even though he'd frightened them, they were told he would still give gifts to good children. There was no tree. No fanfare and or glistening wonder-eyed kids, only hopeful innocence. But when they'd look inside those worn shoe boxes that next morning, that's when the magic happened. What their Santa left for them was more than special: a couple of apples, an orange, a couple walnuts, a Brazil nut, a couple pieces of candy (peppermint or butterscotch), a small toy car for the boys or a little doll for the girls. They were skimpy gifts by any standard, but these were not typically afforded throughout the year, so they were received as extra special treats. This was their joyful Christmas morning, simple and thrilling.

Dad said that in lean times, Poppa Isaac would tell them, "Santa had a wreck at the North Pole, but still put your boxes in front of the fire." There would be less fruit, maybe only one nut, a handmade doll for the girls, and a small car made from a spool of thread with buttons for wheels for the boys. Still, they were thrilled black Santa had come and left them some treats and goodies.

Every year at Christmas at our church the youth would reenact the Christmas story, recite short poems, and join in singing communal carols. The elders of the church—mostly farmers and others who'd grown up in the Frierson and Gayle, Louisiana, sharecropped lands—would prepare a modest brown bag of treats for each of the children that contained a couple pieces of fruit and hard candy, either butterscotch and peppermint. I wondered then why they gave us such meager treats when we wanted the modern toys and the things we'd seen on television. But when I learned later of this simple brown gift bag tradition that had been my father's and most of theirs, I realized that what they were passing down was not simply fruit, candy and nuts in a bag, rather it was given as a remembrance of our forefather's challenges. I also realized there was tremendous joy in the simplicity and profound hand-packed love in each bag.

I thought Santa had forgotten me one year because I didn't receive my big request: a very special bike with white wheels (one small and one large) and a long white banana seat that I had seen shining in a storefront downtown window. It was the prettiest bike I had ever seen, and I wanted it desperately. When I didn't find it on Christmas morning, I felt like maybe I hadn't been worthy of that amazing bike; that I hadn't been "good enough."

After we were done with our gift opening and back in our bedrooms, the doorbell rang. My sister Kathy and I raced to get there and when I opened the door, the bike was waiting for me on the front porch! Overjoyed and elated, I was thrilled to tears. Little did I understand then how my parents had worked hard and saved up extra to give me that very special gift, or why they were always extra tired parents on Christmas mornings. That showroom bicycle was the best gift of my childhood Christmases. Even at twelve, I felt such gratitude for "Santa" granting my wildest wish.

I have tremendous appreciation for the joy and glee our Christmases embodied, and I have great humility and respect for the kind of Christmas my dad was given. Fruit and hard candy were symbols of the best his times could offer. It means so much more now, knowing there was gratitude and love in the little brown bag of treats they gave us at church and in every gift our parents worked to give us.

For all the goodies and presents that symbolize Christmas today, what Dad taught me with all those magical Christmases was that it is really about the act of gifting in reverence to the miracle birth of the baby Jesus, and the token of giving whether grand or meager, brings joy and wonder to your child, to any child. While his Christmas mornings held its own kind of magic, we were his delight and wonder.

Dad would say, "We give you kids some of what we got and hopefully more." He would always remind us to appreciate the true meaning of Christmas; not just about getting gifts, but about giving and to celebrate Jesus's birth. It is through simple traditions and customs that we learn our history. The old mixes with the new, passed down with love and reverence, to remain an integral part of the people we become and the customs we carry forward.

CHAPTER 8
If Six O'clock Be Daylight

———

Everyone started the day in the lot, a dusty square enclosed by a wooden fence where workers hitched and watered the mules. Herman Cannit was one of the overseers on the Frierson plantation in Gayle, Louisiana where my dad's family had moved after leaving their home in Holly. Mr. Arch Frierson had bought up tens of thousands of acres of land for pennies after a huge flood. When the waters receded, he turned that land into cotton fields and a fortune for his family that has lasted generations. There were no machines to do such back-breaking work; the workers were the machines for sowing, planting and harvesting. In 1941 rural Louisiana, black sharecroppers and children worked alongside their parents, siblings and friends as soon as they could hold a hoe. Old and young worked the large plantation fields, plowing the fields, planting the cotton seeds, weeding their rows, chopping, picking, bailing, hauling and loading cotton from sunup to sundown. Their pay? Fifty cents a day.

It wasn't uncommon for the overseer or other whites in power to refer to the black males as "boy." As a young boy, Dad had quietly decided that if someone didn't call him by his name, he reacted by not reacting; he would ignore it as though he didn't hear it. This was, in his own way, his quiet act of civil disobedience.

One day Herman Cannit yelled, "Aye, come here, boy!"

Dad kept on doing what he was doing, not returning a comment or glance.

"You hear me? I say come here, boy!" Dad continued to ignore him, never looking in his direction.

Then Cannit said, "Hey! Goddammit, you hear me?"

Dad looked up calmly. "Who you talking to?" he asked, looking around.

"You!" Cannit thundered.

"I ain't no boy, my name is Green," my dad told him. "That's what my father and mother named me, and you don't know my name. You could say 'man', 'young man', or 'mister', whatever you want to say, but don't call me no boy," he emphatically stated without batting an eye.

"Oh, you want to be smart," Cannit replied.

"Well, I'm not smart, I'm just telling you how I feel."

Herman Cannit rode up to young Green on his big brown horse and told him to be back at the lot, ready to plow and pick up his mule by 6:00 a.m. the next morning. The fourteen-year-old, tall and lanky Green said calmly, "If six o'clock be daylight, I'll be there."

The usual practice was that all the workers would be at the lot by sun up or daylight, but men in Cannit's position could, according to dad, "throw their weight around or pick on somebody." That day he had picked on young Green. Most people just did what they were told and did not question authority, for fear of aggression against them or their family.

It was still dark at six o'clock the next morning, but daylight came soon after. When young Green got his mule, it was seven o'clock and some workers were already plowing. He plowed because it made extra money for his Poppa. At sundown, he put up the mule and was walking with a couple friends down the road when Herman Cannit rode alongside and stopped him.

"Boy, I thought I told you to be at the lot for six o'clock!" he said in a harsh tone.

"And I told you, if six o'clock be daylight, I would be there. I came when it was daylight."

"Who you think you talking to?"

Young Green replied gently, "I'm talking to you."

Cannit motioned as if he was going to get down off his fifteen-hands-high mahogany horse to frighten or do harm to young Green. The lion's mouth of subservience was roaring and fear pricked beneath the skin of his lanky 6'2", frame, and he felt vulnerable and bullied. He was super slim at fourteen, but surprisingly strong and kept pace with and picked more cotton than his much older brothers.

Dad carried a switchblade in his pocket, hoping he never had to use it, but ready if needed. As he slid his hand into his pocket, prepared to protect himself, a rush of confidence filled him, combined with the heart-pounding fight or flight feeling. Young Green who was normally the peacemaker knew he would not be bullied and that he had to stand up for himself. In that moment, he also remembered what his father had taught him, "You don't have to fight, son. If you have to run, do, but if they follow you, you have to fight. Trouble is easy to get into, but hell to get out of."

Still, he stood his ground and looked Cannit directly in the eyes. "If you get off that horse," Green told him, "somebody else gonna put you back up on it. I am not a child. I'm a man and I work as hard as anybody here."

Cannit could see the fire in his eyes and paused before swinging his leg out of the stirrup. He sat back in the saddle, turned and rode away.

Young Green did a slow exhale and inwardly smiled, though he was quite shaky inside from the momentary confrontation with someone of great authority. He had never done anything like that, but remembered that Poppa Isaac had always told them to stand up for what they believed to be right. It felt good and new to speak up and not be so compliant with every rule.

He went home and immediately told his mother what had happened. Though it was unusual for any black person working on a farm to stand up to authority, she told him she was proud of him. But she was also worried that he would be in trouble with Mr. Herman and Mr. Arch.

The following Saturday, Green was called to Arch Frierson's office. The stoutly-built plantation owner standing about five-foot-nine, had a kindly face with twinkly sky blue eyes, salt and pepper hair with spaced yellowish teeth. Mr. Arch gently asked him, "Green, what's wrong with you and Herman? He said you sassed him. I want y'all to all git 'long."

Dad told him, "Ain't nothing, Mr. Arch. He told me to be at the lot for six o'clock. I told him if six o'clock be daylight, I'd be there, but it was still night. I went there at seven and got my mule and I went and plowed."

"Well, he's the overseer, you know," Mr. Arch said.

"Yeah, but he acted like I was his child," dad stated matter-of-factly. "He acted like he wanted to get down off his horse, like he was gon' come and do something to me. And I told him if he got down somebody was gonna pick him up and put him back up there."

Mr. Arch took an exhaled moment. "Well, y'all get along now."

"I get along Mr. Arch, 'cause I don't bother nobody."

After Dad left, he saw Herman Cannit headed to his office. Dad eased back to the door to hear what was said. "Herman, I done told you 'bout messing with them boys," Mr. Arch said, admonishing him. "Somebody gon hang yo' ass, you know?!"

Young Green, tickled and relieved, eased away from the door and went on his way.

Poppa Isaac had a very good relationship with Mr. Frierson. There had been great respect between the them, perhaps because Poppa Isaac's large family provided so much labor and because he was valued as a reliable, highly skilled farm worker. Some would say back then that he was a "good cotton-picking negro." The Whitaker brothers would pick more cotton than most anyone in those parts, and they were highly valuable to the Frierson bottom-line revenue. Mr. Frierson also respected my grandfather because he knew he was a beloved pious man in the community, helpful to all, often standing toe to toe with him on correct payment for the bales his family picked. Because of Poppa Isaac's ability to do math in his head, he could calculate on the spot what they were to be paid. If Mr. Arch gave an arbitrary number to pay them for their work, my grandfather would quickly do the math and show him the correct pay due. Dad said he had heard Mr. Frierson once say laughingly, "Ike, cain't pull nothin' on you!" Dad also said that Poppa Isaac who was known to outwardly show love for his children by hugs, once stopped while having a conversation with Mr. Arch, walked over to the nearby small school and gave each of his children a kiss as they came through the door. Mr. Frierson remarked, "Ike, you sho' love your chi'ren." He replied,

"Sho' do. Ev'ry single one of them."

Dad said Mr. Arch Frierson had a kinder heart than his son, who would take over some years later. Perhaps he had a heart for Ike's boy that day because of the love he had witnessed between them, and maybe he was likely kind and more open to my dad because of that good relationship he had with Ike.

The matter was never brought up again, nor did Herman Cannit ever approach young Green in that way. When my dad told me this story, he admitted that he still didn't know what made him feel so brave that day. "This was a time when a black man didn't have a voice. They could take you out and shoot you and nothing would be done about it and nobody would go to jail. So people were careful to stay in their place for safety's sake," he said.

I'd like to think that my dad was spared any punishment or harm because he had stepped into the grace of his father's standing, or maybe because he had the nerve to stand up like a man, regardless of color, for what he believed was fair. Maybe it softened Mr. Frierson that day to the point that he took the side of a black field worker over his white overseer. They say the favor of your ancestors can carry over to later generations, and this may have been one of those favored moments.

Marker of the old, rural town of Gayle where the Whitaker family moved to and became sharecroppers

CHAPTER 9
Don't Borrow What You Can't Pay Back

Friday was the plantation payday. At week's end, the bales of cotton would be weighed and the workers paid the amount the owner said they'd earned. There was little or no bargaining power. When Dad was around eighteen, he went to "settle up" for the week with Mr. Frierson, the landowner, but he wasn't in his office. The upcoming Sunday was the annual big baptizing day, and Dad planned to use some of his earnings to purchase new Sunday clothes because his were threadbare. There was no one else he could turn to for the money; his brothers had their own clothes to buy, some for their own families, and he would never burden his widowed mother by asking her for money.

Ever since Poppa Isaac died, he had given all he earned to his mother to help keep things going at home. She would always give him a little back for his personal needs, always so grateful, but what she gave back would not cover new Sunday clothes.

Dad heard some men talking in the fields about another farm owner, Roberson Cupper, who would sometimes loan money. A loan shark of his day, rumor was that Mr. Cupper had killed some men who borrowed and did not pay him back. Dad considered this before going to see him, but he took a chance because his intentions were honorable and there wasn't anyone else he felt he could ask.

He entered Mr. Cupper's office, a wood shed on the edge of his property. Mr. Cupper, a rotund man with a ruddy complexion, medium brown eyes, wiry white hair, and a salt and pepper mustache, sat in a dusty office behind a dust-covered metal desk.

"Hello, Mr. Cupper, you don't know me from Adam's housecat," my dad said, introducing himself. "My name is Green Whitaker and I am in need to borrow $20 from you."

"Why you want to borrow from me?" Mr. Cupper asked in a

booming voice.

"I heard you could give a short-term loan. When I went to settle-up with Mr. Frierson, he wasn't in his office. Sunday is our big baptizing day, and I need to get me some new clothes to wear to church. And next Friday when I get paid, I'll come right here and pay you back."

Mr. Cupper thought for a moment as he sat in his denim overalls. His feet, clad in worn boots covered with dried mud, were propped up on the desk, a .45 revolver right next to them.

After several seconds that felt like long minutes, Mr. Cupper finally spoke. "You right, young man, I don't know you from Adam's housecat, but when people don't pay me back, I've been known to make sure they do."

"Well, you won't have to worry about that," Dad assured him.

He paused in thought to consider young Green's words. He stood up. "I'mma let you have it. Bring me the $20 when you catch Mr. Frierson."

Relieved, Dad said happily, "I shole will!"

Mr. Cupper pulled a crisp bill from his pocket and laid the money on the table. Dad picked it up and headed out, thanking him as he left.

The next Friday, Dad again went to Mr. Frierson to settle-up. Again, he was not there. Now he was in the predicament of not having the money to pay Mr. Cupper back through circumstances beyond his control. Fear pulsed through him, because of what he'd heard and what Mr. Cupper had implied. He wondered what he could do or say to Mr. Cupper. After all, he had given his word.

Then he remembered what his daddy had taught him: "When you get something from somebody, you return it to them better than they gave it to you. Secondly, don't borrow what you can't pay back. If you don't have the money to pay back a debt, you go talk to them. Stand up! Don't be a coward; be a man and take responsibility. Go to the person and let 'em know what's going on. It goes a long way in how people see you."

Still anxious, he didn't know how Mr. Cupper would react to

his showing up empty-handed. What would he say? Would he be shot? Punched? He wasn't sure, but knew he had to talk to him and tell him the truth. He wanted to do the right thing, as his daddy had taught him. He asked his mother for advice and she echoed what his father had told him, agreeing that it was better to go and explain what happened instead of not saying anything at all.

To Mr. Cupper's he went, praying and trying to steady his fast-beating heart as he approached his office. He walked in and was greeted with a "Hey there, Green. You come to bring me my money?" Mr. Cupper looked up at him with his ruddy face and coffee-stained teeth. The revolver sat prominently on his desk.

"Yes, sir. But I don't have it," Dad said, hoping Mr. Cupper would see the honesty in his words.

Mr. Cupper began to sit forward. "I went to settle up and Mr. Frierson was gone again," Dad continued. "I've come to let you know that is the only reason I don't have your money."

Mr. Cupper took this in while Dad held his breath. "Green, you done just what you said. What you did, coming here to talk to me, is just like paying me back. You stood up like a man. That's what I call being a man. I know yo daddy proud of ya. Look here, no rush. Whenever you catch ol' Arch, you come and pay me then."

"I thank you, sir," Dad said.

The relief he felt was immeasurable. More than that, he felt a sense of pride and honor for doing the very thing his father had taught him; be honest and face your debtors instead of dodging them.

The very next week, when Dad did catch Mr. Frierson, he got his money and went directly to Mr. Cupper to pay his debt in full. Mr. Cupper didn't charge him any interest. Though he never needed to borrow money again from him, the lesson of being mindful of what you borrow and that you pay it back was a lesson hard earned and hard learned.

CHAPTER 10

I Was Cut Out For It, But Wasn't Sewed Up Right

Around the age of nineteen, his brother LeRoy ("Uncle Roy"), and their close friend Buddy Richmond were driving home to Gayle from town. The packed dirt roads looked more like worn wide trails as they drove in a black '36 Ford with a "mother-in-law seat"—an exterior upholstered bench seat that folded into the rear of the car--- when suddenly, the car broke down in a wooded area at dusk.

The three of them got out to try to fix the car. Uncle Roy was a fun-loving, handsome, honey-colored man with wavy black hair and thin mustache who resembled my dad but stood nearly a head shorter. Uncle Roy had heaps of style, good looks and could get the prettiest girls. With a quick smile, high cheekbones and a strong jawline, he greeted people warmly with "Hey, good liver!" Though he was hard-working, Uncle Roy was equally hot-headed, always ready for a fight, while my dad's first inclination was to make peace. He was the cooling salve to his fiery furnace; they were yin and yang, contrary forces that complemented each other perfectly.

While they were trying to fix the car, a stockily built black man stepped out from behind a tree and confronted them, mostly talking to Uncle Roy. "I hear you trying to see my girl," he said accusingly.

"She don't belongs to you. And I can see anybody I please," Roy boldly replied.

My dad began looking at Uncle Roy, signaling him to calm down and play nice. The man stepped forward and said more forcefully, "I'm telling you to stop messing with my girl!"

Uncle Roy bristled. "Seem like she don't think she your girl 'cause she seeing me." He was immediately puffed up and ready to fight, not backing down at all.

"Roy, you need to simmer down!" Dad whispered under his

breath. Then he turned to the man, taking the lead. "Listen, we just trying to get home. We don't want no trouble. Just as soon as we get the car going, we will be on our way."

With his eyes locked on Uncle Roy, the man said in a menacing tone, "You know, me and my boys could take you out right now."

The man pointed to the woods and snapped his fingers. Four armed men stepped from behind different trees (like you see in an ambush on the old TV show Gunsmoke). "But because of Preacher man here," he said, with a quick flick of his chin and a nod to Dad, his eyes squarely on Uncle Roy, "I'mma let you go this time."

My dad looked around. "Who, me?"

"Yeah, you a preacher?" the man asked.

"Well, I was cut out for it, but wasn't sewed up right," he replied, in a moment of revelation as much to himself as to the man.

That made the man giggle a bit, and lightened the situation. "You better be glad I respect him," he retorted, keeping his gaze on Uncle Roy. "But let this be your warning to stay 'way from my girl."

The men quietly retreated into the woods as quickly as they had appeared. Dad breathed a sigh of relief; they all could have been killed. My dad shot Uncle Roy a side-eyed look. You'd better not say a mumbling word! Inside, he was shaking like a leaf in the wind.

They got the car started and headed home, shaken by the whole ordeal. My dad's persona and reputation as a godly man had saved the day, along with whatever angels were hovering about to keep those brother men from an ambush.

Dad knew the ways of the times. He knew that he couldn't be too bold, because a black man in the Jim Crow South with no judicial support didn't have much of a leg to stand on or anyone to whom he could complain. He learned how to manage around the existing system. His character and kindness to others spoke volumes.

This was not the last time my dad was mistaken for a preacher; it has happened many times throughout his life. When we were young kids, Dad insisted that my mother not cook on Sundays, a traditional day of rest— her one day off from making home- cooked meals for the family, in addition to working her full-time job as a librarian. On

Sundays, Dad would treat us to dinner at the Big Chain Cafeteria, a buffet-style eatery with separate seating for "coloreds" and "whites." I was young and unaware that we were sitting in a designated area.

My dad's love, affectionate gestures, and chivalrous manners were constants. He always opened doors for my mother and stood until all us girls were seated. At the restaurant, he always made a plate first for my brother, got him seated and comfortable before fixing his own. We kids were dressed in our Sunday best at the restaurant, coming from church, and we were always well behaved, in restaurants anyway.

One day, Dad recalls, a white lady crossed the ropes separating the sections, came over to him, and put her hand on his shoulder. When he first noticed her heading toward our table, he felt uneasy. This was a most unusual gesture as the whites didn't mix with the blacks, and they certainly didn't come over and touch one they didn't know. He said under his breath to Mom, "Lord, what in the world is this lady coming over here for? Did we do or say something?"

He quickly replaced that gentle worry with a kind smile when she stood right next to him at our table. She said to dad, "I travel all over and I see a lot of people but I haven't seen anyone quite like you. The love you show for them is so beautiful. And your family is beautiful. I just had to come tell y'all. Are you a preacher? Have you been called?"

My dad looked around sheepishly taking this in. "Well, I ain't heard nothing yet." A splendid reply.

She smiled with warm eyes. "You might have a calling. Bless y'all," and walked back to her table.

That was another example of his "preacher" essence once again granting him grace — and a genuinely nice compliment to boot. Perhaps it was the way Dad carried himself, his tall slim stature and suited Sunday attire, or his devotion to God that spilled out in his interactions with everyone. It served him well and garnered good will, as well as getting him out of a few rough spots. Sometimes, he says, "The things people think you represent can be an asset for good. Somewhere in what they see can be some truth about something within you that you can't yet see." '

Who knows what moved that lady to come and talk to my dad. Whatever it was, she saw something that was always present and yet effortless for him—a deep abiding love for his family, exemplified in all he did.

But for all the times that Dad was the voice of reason or calm, there were other times when, because of circumstances, he lost his hard earned composure. One of those times was when he and my mother made a double date to meet at the movies (sitting, of course, in the black section) with Uncle Roy and Aunt Lillian who brought along their baby daughter. Uncle Roy having gotten off work was still in his work clothes and steel hard hat. Two sisters had married two brothers. As soon as they settled into their seats, a group came in and sat in the row behind them. It was obvious they were drinking because they were passing a bottle of brown liquor between them and becoming rowdier and rowdier. One said something about them bringing a baby to the movies which they all ignored. When the woman slumped down in her seat, her knees pushed into Uncle Roy's arm that hugged Aunt Lillian's shoulders.

The women commented loudly, "Mister, git yo' hands outta my lap."

Aunt Lillian replied with, "It's not in your lap. If you sat up right, then nobody would have their hand in yo lap".

Then man said, "That's alright, I'll make 'em move it." Things quickly escalated from there and when one of the men went to hit Uncle Roy with the bottle, he drew back to retaliate but the woman stepped in between them and caught the punch. The fight was on and Uncle Roy's steel hat was ringing "Bling, Bling, Bling" as he whipped the man with it. The woman pulled out a metal nail file and struck him on the temple and blood streamed down his face. During the fight, the other man in the group lunged and grabbed Dad around the neck. Quickly he pulled the man over the seat, frisked him, then proceeded to "work that head ova!" with punches. Then the woman turned towards Dad.

"Ma'am go back Lady, don't come up on me!" he warned her

but when she didn't retreat Dad said he, "turned loose" on her. "I told you don't come ova here!" he chided. Because he had been taught that a gentleman should never hit a lady, he was not proud that he had had to. Dad was not cut out for that or felt sewed up right in that situation, but he also realized that when the situation arose, he did what he had to do.

CHAPTER 11

You Got Wings

I wanted to know more about my dad's experience of being a cotton picker; to understand the step by step details of the process from seed to bale. I wanted to understand what the experience was like as well as his thoughts and feelings while working in the fields picking the unique fluffy white fiber substance that had been the backbone of the American economy in the 19th century. I interviewed him during one of my visits back home.

"How did it start, Daddy?" I asked.

He began by telling me that in April, each worker in his family (and most of the plantation workers in that area) hitched up a mule with a planter attached. "The land had already been broken up and plowed a few days before and each of the parallel rows of soil was built up in the middle with several holes to drop the seeds into. Then we guided the mule over the row 'and the planter was gauged to drop two or three seeds in each hole. After that, the work was to keep those rows clean of weeds, grass and vines so that when the buds came up, they didn't kill the bolls. And when it got hot enough, the stalk shot up looking like an okra plant." Dad said everyone kept their hoes razor sharp each day with a sharpening file. "You'd have to chop the grass 'round that stalk that come up like "hair on a poodle's back." The grass and vines would have to be hoed and chopped every day."

Back-breaking work, but everyone he knew did it.

"Life was a little different then," he recounted. "We would plow, hoe, chop, or pick, in its season most days, and we tried our best to go to school. My sisters and mother would work until 'leven in the fields, then go in to prepare lunch for our family. The bell would ring at noon, and we'd go in to eat a home-cooked meal after we'd washed up a bit. Then, if we had any time left, we'd fall out and lay around on the porch; just a little break, maybe a short nap. The bell would ring at 1 o'clock and then we'd work 'til sundown. It was so hot some days in the field, but you just kept on working. We come up on the rough side, but thank God we made it."

His pride and assuredness shone through as he continued. "In June, the cotton stalk would come up tall, about two or three feet high. When we had hard rains, I saw the cotton so tall, you couldn't see a man on a horse riding through," Dad remembered. "When it got hot enough and the plant got a certain size, eight to ten bolls (the cotton's protective shell) on a stalk would turn from green to yellow to brown and open up to reveal the white cotton. That's when the picking began."

Daddy took me through the next steps of the process — the six-foot burlap "foot sack," a long cloth receptacle that held the cotton as it was picked. From how he described it, the thinnest part of the sack, its handle, was draped over the head like a long cross-body bur-lap bag that dragged on the ground. A tar-like material was applied to the bottom of the bag so you wouldn't drag a hole in your sack as you picked the cotton down the row. The details came quickly, as if Dad were still standing in the field: "The opened bolls had thorny ends that could prick the finger but you picked anyway; pick the cotton, throw it in the sack, shake it down and repeat 'til the sack was full."

I asked him if it was quiet, or if any chatting or singing went on when the work was happening. He told me there were minimal con-versations, but most were focused on filling those sacks. "Some days, my Momma and the other ladies would hum or sing while they were picking—songs like 'When I Get Home' and 'What a Great Gettin' Up Morning!' and 'Bye and Bye, When the Morning Comes!'

"Momma would say, 'Alright now! Y'all gon' start something!' Sometimes they would catch the Holy Ghost and start shouting on their row or at the end of the row, and you'd see dust kicking up as they shouted."

His father sometimes created games to break up the monoto-ny of the work and to keep the boys motivated. Knowing they were competitive, Poppa Isaac sometimes made it a race to see who got to the end of their row first; or whose stalks had the first buds, all with small monetary prizes. He laughed as he recalled all this. In spite of the hard work, they seemed to find moments to rejoice in each other, and hope for better days to come. Some of his older brothers and sisters were getting married and starting families of their own and Dad could see that some of them wanted more for their growing families too.

Dad also told me that the workers were not informed about the seed or purchase price of the crop they labored to harvest. After the cotton was picked, it was put on a sheet to weigh and they were paid "fifty cents on 100 pounds." If prices changed, they were never told how much it increased. They had to take what they were given, with no other recourse to oppose or ask what they were being paid. They just had to accept it.

A bale typically weighed 470 pounds (500 pounds was considered a big bale). When I was trying to figure out what that looked like, I learned that a 500-pound bale of cotton can produce 800 dresses, 325 pairs of jeans, 1,200 pillowcases, or 313,000 hundred-dollar bills. Since cotton is light and weighs very little, the sheer height of the cotton it took to make a bale must have stood taller than six feet.

I asked Dad if there was anything about picking cotton that he enjoyed; if there were any big lesson he learned, and his first reply was "I'd never ever go back to the days of picking cotton, that's for sho, but it was the life we all had, and we made the best of it. Only the family working together and the home life, that was the good part. Everybody did this field work, this half hand, where half of what you worked for was given to the owner of the land," he recounted. "After our daddy died, we all worked extra hard to help Momma 'round the house with things she needed and expenses. That's how we were raised; when you get up to do a little better, you reach back and help take care of ya' parents."

In trying to help their mother stay ahead of expenses, when they were sixteen and seventeen, he and his brother Leroy, worked ten extra acres one year on Mr. Arch Frierson's land. The harvest produced twelve bales of cotton to make extra money. Mr. Arch got six of it, while they kept six working "half hands." When they went to settle-up with him, Mr. Arch said, "Well, boys, you done good."

Dad and his brother waited patiently for the big pay day, for which they had worked all year. "The pay for this is $75," Mr. Arch said, which was to be split between the two of them.

"Mr. Arch, this don't seem right. For 12 bales we picked, this seems low," my dad said.

Mr. Arch tried to convince them. "You know, I try to do right by my people", he started to explain. "I have to get horses and mules, buy seed, and keep things up around here."

Still, my dad insisted that the math wasn't right and that they were not responsible for his overhead expenses. "We didn't take up nothin' on this crop," he said, meaning they didn't borrow any money for seed or other expenses, so why should they bear the burden of Mr. Frierson's overhead?

As mentioned earlier, at that time, and for many decades prior, these hard-working black men had no voice nor recourse, which left many of them without a choice beyond being unemployed or accepting what was given.

Disgusted and knowing they were cheated, Dad went home and told his mother about the short pay from the twelve bales and that he and his brother did not want to pick cotton or work for Mr. Frierson anymore.

She thought about it, then said, "Well, Mr. Arch has been alright boys, he has work for y'all. You should try another year."

Because they were obedient sons, they went back for the next season. This time, they yielded thirteen bales — 6 ½ for them and the same for Mr. Arch. Again, he said, "Well, boys, y'all done real good this year." When they settled up, he gave them only $125 for the year's work. Though it was more than the previous year, the pay was arbitrary from year to year, season to season. Dad and Uncle Roy knew the pay was still unfair and much less than it should have been. They could have figured it out with paper and pencil had he had the numbers to calculate, none of which they were ever given.

Dad looked at that meager pay and knew without a doubt he was done working for that man. In the face of being cheated time and time again over the years, he finally decided to step away. He had to do that work for a time to get himself ahead and because that's what he knew how to do, but his eyes were focused a bit farther away from the only work life he'd known. Green had had enough.

What had started with my simple question while on a basic fact-finding mission, turned into a much clearer understanding of the systemic racism that limited what black people could own, the kinds of jobs they could have, the oppression of having to choose work over getting an education, and the prejudice my dad and black people endured. I felt such a boiling rage for that time and how he managed to maneuver around the system set up to keep him in his subordinate place in the pre-civil rights movement.

My dad said calmly, "There come a time in a man's life where you know you've done enough, had enough, and it's time to change, move on. Most people get comfortable in the way thangs is, but there is always a small voice telling you, it's time. Time for a change. That happened to me a few times in my life, but this was a big one." A voice in Dad's head said to him, "You don't have to stay, you got wings!"

He contemplated the deeper meaning of these words and thought out loud. "Ya, see, just like the caterpillar that will eat cotton leaves, and when he gets tired, he web himself up and goes through a change and come out a butterfly! See, we can change and be more than what we were." That's exactly what he did. When he was eighteen, he told his mother he was going to town to see if he could find a job. Since she wanted her sons always to leave the light on and a door open in their work relationships, she asked him to tell Mr. Arch that he was quitting. When he did so, Mr. Arch asked, "Whatcha gon' do, Green?" knowing he didn't have other skills and had not been able to finish his education because of work and helping support his mother.

Then he made Dad an offer. "You can come back here to work if it don't work out," he said, in his somber slow drawl.

Dad thought to himself, If I have to come back, I shole as heck won't come back here! But he ended with a gesture of kindness, "I thank you."

Dad bid Mr. Arch a good day and never looked back. He got a

part-time job at Caddo Casket Company, and later worked on the railroad, driving spikes from Shreveport down to Red Shoot, Louisiana. Some of the Whitakers (uncles and other male cousins) had developed a reputation for being fighters. It was known in those parts not to mess with Ike's boys, but others were pistol toting, righteous men willing to defend their family and their dignity.

When I heard this story, I felt my anger rise. I asked Dad how he could be so kind after all that he and his family had endured. I wanted to understand how he could not be full of the rage I was feeling as I listened to these stories where he was repeatedly getting cheated doing backbreaking work, being overworked, and underpaid; the indignation of it all and the idea of his entire family, my family doing this hard labor work and not being paid commensurately.

"Baby girl," he said, "My faith in God got us all through it, and we were all in there together, so it was happening to us all at once. And when it's all you know, you don't have anything to compare it to." Daddy wasn't angry at all. He had gained and earned an incredible work ethic and had life skills to last more than a couple lifetimes. My anger bent to sadness, then to great pride as I now understood the courage, the resilience and smarts it took to survive, the intuitive kindness and common sense he used to tame the lion of oppression that was all around him and the tools he possessed to make it through the world he was born into.

However, the small voice that spoke to him that day gave him the motivation to make more of a life than he had been born into. "You gotta keep pushing yourself" he said, and reminded me that just because a thing happened to you doesn't mean it is all that you are. We are not defined by our circumstances.

Next, I asked him what happened after he left working on the plantation and later married Mother. I wanted to know if he ever picked cotton again. He told me that it wasn't until he married our mother and was working at Alan Millwork, that he learned how much they had been taken for granted and underpaid. He was twenty-one or twenty-two and wanted to pick up some extra work and income. A gentleman named Cal Fife, who had a reputation of being a fair man, had a cotton field in town near where Daddy and Mother were living.

Mr. Fife was looking for someone to keep his ten acres clean, to hoe and pick it. Dad hired four or five people to pick with him, paying them what he had been paid, 50 cents per 100 pounds of cotton. He also hired someone with a trailer to weigh it. He was still on the railroad full-time, so this was his side job. "First year, we made 12 bales of cotton. Mr. Fife handed me a check for $1,000, plus gave us seed money that was another $200! I told my wife, 'Look at this!'"

He worked another season for Mr. Fife. For the first time in that kind of work, Dad saw a fair, decent man in how he treated his workers and how he paid them. That was the last time he ever picked cotton. "I got my wings now, and I was gone from those cotton-picking days!" Dad told me with glee. I giggled.

I marvel at my Dad's resilience and kindness to come through such a hard road. His resolve in surviving and getting out of it was absolute. He has said to me and my siblings many times, "If you find yourself doing something you don't like, you don't have to stay. Be like that caterpillar who becomes a butterfly. Get your wings and fly!"

The cotton plantation where the Whitaker family worked

CHAPTER 12
He Just Knew
———

Some things you just know. That's what Daddy said about the first time he saw the back of her thick, shoulder-length, pressed, black-haired head. He just knew. On a hot and muggy night, he laid eyes on her, leaned forward to the bench below and, without any personal exchange or prior interaction, tapped her on the shoulder. When she turned to see who was doing the tapping, he whispered-shouted, "I'm gon' marry you!"

He saw her at a gathering at what was then called a "sanctified church." A Reverend William Young, a sanctified preacher, had converted a large white house near the end of White Springs Road where her family lived, into a church. Sanctified was the Pentecostal tradition characterized by a more experiential faith with the gifts of the Spirit such as speaking in tongues, prophecy and healing. Much later it became Church of God in Christ, or COGIC.

Wooden slats were arranged in a smaller stadium seating style, where a more relaxed suit-wearing men and breezy Sunday dressed women sat shoulder to shoulder during a late afternoon service; the air was punctuated with familiar hand claps and shouts outs of "Say that!" or "Thank ya, Jesus!", or "Amen, Preacher!" Heels tapped on the plywood floors, in rhythm with the spirit-filled congregational songs. Union and community flowed through this church service.

Sixteen-year-old Ola Mae White, her hair pulled into a low ponytail that contrasted her smooth coffee bean-colored skin, shooed him away with a flick of her wrist. "There's already one Whitaker dating my sister," she whisper-shouted back.

He leaned forward to say "He ain't me!"

My dad had said out loud that he wasn't gonna to marry "anybody's daughter" simply because of the pressure put on the young men by their communities to get married young. He was having none of that. But in that knowing moment, Ola Mae was the one who instantly changed his mind. For him, she was the one.

Within a few weeks of that first encounter, he set out to win her heart. It was expected for a gentleman caller to ask permission to date a young lady and he worked up the nerve to ask her father, Mr. "Buddy" White. "I'd like to talk with you, sir. Do you have any objection to me comin' to see your daughter?" Buddy was known for both his gentleness and being a man of few but rapidly spoken words. He was also fiercely protective of his daughters. Ola Mae, who was the eldest of fifteen children, helped her mother stay on top of the chores and her younger siblings coming up behind her. Lillian, her eleven-month younger sister was already dating his younger brother Leroy.

"Come 'round to see her for what?" Buddy said rapidly in a high-pitched voice.

Dad, tall and scrawny at six-foot-two and around 145 pounds, looked down at Mr. Buddy. He wanted to have the right answer, so he could unlock the portal to spend some time with Ola Mae.

"I would like to get to know her, sir, I think she's a special girl," Dad replied.

Buddy called out to his wife, my grandmother, who was inside the house. "Loisee?! This boy here says he wanna date Mae!"

Mudea (as her kids called her), came in and said, "Well, Buddy, he is a nice young man and I don't have any objection."

Buddy continued, "Whatchu wanna date her for?"

Dad was surprised by the question. "Well, sir, I . . . I like her a lot."

Buddy, standing with some distance between them, was about five-foot-eleven, slender and with velvety dark chocolate skin and shining clear dark eyes. He was quiet for a moment, thinking. Then he called out to Mamma Hattie, my great grandmother who lived with them to learn what she thought about it all.

"Mamma Hattie, come in here. This boy say he wanna see Mae. What you think about it? She too said she thought it he was a nice man and gave no objections.

As we say in the south, "Tap a shoulder but pat a foot." Buddy patted his foot for what felt like an eternity, then he spit on the ground.

"Ummm-huh," he said, thinking out loud in the pause. "I heard you Whitakers believe in a man having many wives," he responded, referencing a distant Whitaker cousin who had, in fact, three wives and three different families.

Dad was quick to put his mind to rest. "No, sir! That's just one and he don't represent me." He made it clear that polygamy certainly was not something he nor anyone in his family believed in.

"Everybody for his own", Dad reminded him that he was not any semblance of that distant cousin.

And their courtship began.

They dated for two and a half years and Dad started talking to her about marriage.

On Sundays, he'd walk with her to church as both of her parents strode between them. Privacy was not something they were afforded, but it was enough for them to just be together.

As time and their courtship progressed, Green and Ola Mae talked of getting married. Though she was finishing her high school education and planned to go to college, Dad knew he had to ask her parents for her hand in marriage.

Her response initially was, "I don't know 'bout that. You'll have to talk to my dad." When my Dad would come by their house, he was perplexed to find that each time, Mr. Buddy was not home. A grassy lane led to their home, and as Dad approached, he'd greet whichever family member he saw on the porch or in the front yard. Later, he learned that her father, after hearing his voice outside, would lace up his shoes and head into the woods out back of the house.

He tried coming by every Sunday for three months after church to ask for Poppa Buddy's blessing. Again, suspecting what young Green wanted, Poppa Buddy would head out the back door when he heard Dad coming in the front doors of their small three-bedroom home.

Finally, Dad figured out his strategy. One late afternoon, instead of going to the front door as dusk painted the sky shades of pink and grey, Dad headed to the back and found Poppa Buddy trying to make yet another escape. Dad surprised him with one boot laced and the other not, and prepared to ask that most important question as sincerely as he knew how.

"Mr. Buddy, I'd like to talk with you. Would you have any objection to me marrying your daughter?" he said earnestly.

"What you know 'bout marriage, Green?! She bout to finish school and needs to go to college" Poppa Buddy retorted. "Sir, I will make sure she continues to college." Dad assured him.

"Why you wanna marry her?!"

"Well, I love her." Dad told him.

"Well you said the right thing, now if you can do it", he snapped.

"How you gon' take care of her?"

"I'm gon' work! Whatever it takes, I'll do it to take care of her."

"You don't know nothin' 'bout no marriage. I gotta talk to my wife. Loisee!" he called out. "This boy says he wanna marry Mae. What you think 'bout that?" he said in his fast-talking, stumbling-over-words kind of way.

After a moment, she spoke up in her knowing way. "They love each other, Buddy. And he has been a good kind young fella, so it's okay with me." He again called for Momma Hattie to ask her opinion as they all stood in the small living room. "What y'all say?" She too gave her consent saying he was a "fine young man".

Poppa Buddy turned and asked his daughter, "Life is not an easy thing. If you make your bed hard, you gotta lay in it. Now, do you wanna get married?"

"Yes sir. I do." Daddy said they put him through the first, second, and third degree drills but he understood in the moment that it was about the love for their daughter. An uncomfortable pause followed, then Poppa Buddy said, "And what about all them wives?" he asked pointedly. Without missing a beat, Dad said, "I want just one. This one. That's all." Poppa Buddy walked away saying he wanted to think about it, leaving Dad without an answer. Because of Dad's respect for her father and his sense of chivalry, and the code of ethics, my mom and dad knew they would not be able to move forward without her father's blessing. He made them wait three weeks before he finally gave it.

They were married on December 25, 1947. She had $3 and Dad had $5. But they didn't care. Dad said he wanted to marry someone who had as little as he did so they could grow together, which is exactly what they did. My dad loved her family like his own and wanted Mother to be available for them. He told her, "You have a mother and a father, I only have a mother, so whatever they need I won't hesitate to help them like I would my own." He honored her father's place in his wife's heart.

My grandfather watched how my dad indeed took care of his daughter; how their life and love grew, and that his integrity, love and devotion was admirable. After they were married and Poppa Buddy got to really see the character of my father, he said in dad's presence, "I think this old boy gone be good! He is my best son-in-law!" Early in their marriage, Dad told me that one time he was going to do the dishes as our mother had asked, but got busy outside. When he came in, she asked him why he hadn't and before he could get the answer, she hauled off and slapped him. He grabbed her hand and told her, "Now, if I hit you back, you'll tell your parents I mistreated you. Don't ever do that again." And from that moment until the day she died, Dad said, "never a lick passed between us." My parents discussed things and if they had harsh words between them, they kept it between them. We never saw or heard them argue.

As an observant child, I watched how my parents interacted. I learned without being told but witnessed what a good man is and the way I—and all women—deserve to be treated.

Dad can't quite put into words why he knew my mother was his intended. All that matters is that he knew. But it really doesn't matter because theirs was a bond and union that would inform my choice of partner in the future, showed me what a loving partnership looked like which also gave me a deep sense of well-being and feeling loved. Together they created a family unit built solidly on faith, mutual respect, shared goals, and unconditional love.

The road to Buddy White's family home

CHAPTER 13

Dogs Barking And Biting Nobody But You

I loved the Sundays of my childhood for many reasons, but mostly because the whole family was together for most of the day and because there was lots of music at church. When I was in elementary school, we would leave church for what mother called "pop calls," where we'd drop in to see family that lived in that area including both paternal and maternal grandparents. By the time I was born, my grandfathers had died, so I never got to know either of them, but both grandmothers lived not far from where the church was located.

Sometimes, we kids would get to practice driving on the two-laned asphalt highway. We'd take turns on different Sundays sitting behind the wheel on Dad's lap until our feet could reach the gas and brake pedals. He'd simply say, "Hold it on the road," as our small hands gripped the shiny brown steering wheel at 10 o'clock and 2 o'clock, trying to keep the car between the grassy shoulder and the bright yellow double lines. If the car veered one way or another too much, Dad would remind us to stay in the lane and move us back into the center with his hand gently steering from below.

Big Momma lived down White Springs Road, a long dirt and gravel road, a ten-minute drive from the church. It was named that because of the many natural springs bubbling up from the earth and because my mother's family, the Whites, had owned a lot of the land along that meandering road. I remember the sound of the tires as they turned off the asphalt road and crushed over gravel, which signaled that we were turning onto her road. It ran about four miles from start to finish, dotted with infrequent houses showcasing lush green pastures or farms around them. Chickens roamed freely, cattle grazed, pigs snorted; the swamps and wooded forest were filled with possums, armadillos, raccoons, and other wild species that called the place home and often darted across the road. Sometimes, in the right season, there'd be wild tangled blackberry bushes and wild raspberries on the roadside. We'd stop and pick some, staining our hands and lips, taking some but not all. Occasionally we'd pick from a roadside tree heavy with delicious plums warmed from their sunbath, their taut purple skins popping as we bit into the tart and sweet yellow inside them. As we passed, some of the houses were hidden down narrow dirt lanes with a grassy center off the road and beyond a set of trees, while others were visible from the road.

Big Momma's house was a small three-bedroom off-white wooden structure set on cinder blocks with a corrugated tin A-frame roof, an outhouse in back, and a wood burning stove in the kitchen. The weathered wood front porch, a wood beam at its apex, was half the width of the front of the house, with four two-foot long spaced planks for stairs. Once, I scraped my shin to the white meat when my foot slipped through the space in the steps. The other half was part of a bedroom with a window that looked out onto the sparse dirt and grass lot. The cars parked on some of it. On the small porch sat a seasoned wood slat rocking chair, and in the yard a couple of free-roaming turkeys gobbled, while chickens and a mean old hen trolled the grounds with tall sparse trees above. A forest of trees filled the land just across the road and to the right and left of Big Momma's property. When I spent the night, I learned there was a nearly full "slop jar" if you had to go to the bathroom at night. One of my least fond memories. It felt frozen in time and a world away from our home just a fifteen-minute drive up to the city. Still I loved going there because of the love, food and hugs she gave us all, and because she still had an ice box and wood burning stove.

She was always so happy to see us, offering some manner of cake or pie in her kitchen when we arrived. There was a small dirt road incline to drive onto her property and another house about 100 yards apart where my Uncle Booker T. and his family lived in a smaller house with a steel rain silo to its right.

Before we got to her place, we had to pass by a house painted dark red. We always knew some loud teeth-showing, brown dogs would run out, barking wildly and chasing our car. They would run alongside the car for a few seconds, as though in a race with us, then fall back without fail, and bark and bark and bark. It was always a shock how their bark would startle us kids, even when we knew it was coming.

Another time, when we were on foot and a couple bicycles, we were headed with my cousins to pick up eggs for our grandmother from the "egg man" who sold them. She didn't have a coop and the chickens she had were for eating. Despite how quiet we tried to be as we tiptoed by the red house, holding our breath, those same dogs came tearing out for us. My cousin, Donald Ray saved me by scooping me up on his bike. I don't know if they ever bit anyone, but I also wasn't trying to find out. Most people we knew didn't have indoor dogs; they lived outdoors and roamed free, or under the house when it was cold. Our beloved dog, Skinny, was like that, barking to warn us, but also biting some people who had been aggressive with her. Some dogs bark and some bite, I learned early on. Today our dogs eat, sleep and live indoors, and go to dog parks or leashed walks.

And some dogs, as my Dad says, are also our tired feet.

When my dad and mom got married in 1947, he was twenty-one and she was nineteen. They were just beginning a new life together off the farm, and there wasn't extra money to be had. Their pooled meager savings would go toward their first apartment's rent. Dad had work shoes and Sunday shoes, and both were too worn to wear to a wedding, so he borrowed a newer shiny pair from his brother LeRoy, a snappy dresser—but LeRoy had smaller feet. He had saved some money for a nice suit, but shoes were not in the budget. Dad figured since the wedding would only be ten minutes or so, he could just endure the too-small shoes for that time.

The Reverend Desiree Chipee', a full-blooded African living in those parts, was a churchgoing man who had befriended Mom and Dad. He presided over their wedding ceremony, which unexpectedly lasted two hours. Each time they thought he was at the end, the reverend would say, "Let us pray!" and carry on and on with a prayer.

Meanwhile, Daddy's feet and toes were becoming numb from

the lack of circulation in the too-small shoes. Reverend Chipee' prayed nearly ten times during the ceremony, and each time he added another prayer, a little bead of sweat would pop out on Dad's forehead as he tried to smile through the pain in his feet. Inside the shoes, his toes were curled under, and the pain of his cramped feet pressed on his mind. Mom kept squeezing his hand, because she didn't quite know what was the matter with him, but sensed something was amiss. By the time the reverend finally said, "I now pronounce you man and wife," Dad couldn't feel his feet, but there was a new excitement for the relief to come, because not only were they married, but he could change into his worn Sunday shoes for the after gathering. He heaved a big sigh of relief when the ceremony was done. One of his brothers asked him how he felt about being now married. "My dogs were barking and biting nobody but me!" he quipped.

When I've worn a too-tight, bumping-my-toes-trying-to-be-cute shoe, I remembered those words. When I saw some of my friends struggling in a high heel, or noticed the pain of a pump, a boot, or other cute "ten-minute shoes" or saw the painful stride and knew they could not wait to get out of them, I reached back and grabbed one of Dad's sayings. "Chile, your dogs are barking and bitin' nobody but you!"

*Uncle Booker T. Whitaker, (lived next door
to Big Momma), Aunt Margaret,
and the cousin who saved me, Donald Ray (Beaver)*

CHAPTER 14
Stop Looking

Early in their marriage, Mom and Dad wanted to get ahead financially to be able to better take care of their young family, which then
included their one son who'd been born prematurely and was having
some health and mobility issues. Dad watched a woman drive to his
work each day, her trunk full of hamburgers and small pies for the
workers to buy for lunch. He saw an opportunity to get some additional income and asked if he could also bring some food to sell.
"Why not, Green?! You can make some of that money," his boss said
approvingly.

He talked it over with Mother — and a plan was hatched. They
began by making small sweet potato and condensed milk pies at night
before bed. Then they'd get up at 5:00 a.m. to cook fresh seasoned
hamburgers to also sell. They were meticulous in their preparation;
each burger had mayonnaise, mustard, lettuce, and pickles and was
wrapped in wax paper.

He started small, bringing just a few of their goods to test the
waters. Being a gentleman, he didn't want to assume all the workers
would want to buy their food. He also wanted to be respectful of
the lady who had been selling her goods first, so they set themselves
apart. Mom's pies and burgers were so flavorful that the workers
wanted more and more of hers and Dad became the go-to person for
lunch.

Dad and Mom didn't own a car, so he walked to work each
day (nearly two miles) with his goods to sell. He carried everything
in a discarded large cardboard box that he'd found at the A&P grocery store. They lined it with used egg cartons they'd saved to create
layered rows inside so the burgers, and pies would not be crushed.
He wrapped Mother's old raincoat snugly around the box to protect
the freshly made food from rainy weather and to keep it insulated.

He made handles on each side of the box from rope, then walked a mile and a half to work each morning carrying that box. The load was always lighter going home.

Some of the workers made fun of him. "Green, you're carrying that box every day and then working? Man, you doin' too much!" they teased.

His reply was simple. "You ain't me. If what I'm doing worries you, stop looking!"

Soon, my parents made as much from the sale of burgers and pies as Dad made weekly at his regular job. Those same fellas who teased him would knock on his door on Fridays desperate to borrow some money after not being so wise with their own. Again, Dad saw a way to earn some extra income. He wrote down their names on a pad that Mother kept and loaned them money, charging 50% interest or fifty-cents on a dollar. He stored the paid-back interest in a separate metal lockbox tucked under the living room couch, which became more savings and a bank to loan from. The next time they borrowed, Dad said, "they were borrowing their own money."

With the extra income from lunch sales and interest, Saturday turned into a day of rest and doing family things instead of another day of work to make ends meet. Their hard work during the week gave them a respite, and Dad wasn't worried about what working hard looked like to others. He focused on providing for his family's survival and well-being, especially with a growing little boy who had special needs.

It was a prosperous time. The money didn't make them rich, but it gave them some breathing room. Dad's insight, work ethic, partnership with our mother, and the courage to tote and sell those simple pies and burgers against some taunting, resulted in a better life for their young family. Perhaps it was the initial spark that allowed him and my mother to become role models. They were admired and revered in their growing community and church. Dad said that any-thing was better than those cotton-picking days. This was gravy. Life felt good and blessed.

CHAPTER 15

Find A Way

My parents' life together began with a sweet love and looking forward to creating a home together. They were then devastated by the loss of their first two infant daughters born a year apart, Elaine and Elyse. Both were born prematurely in the fifth month of gestation; Elaine lived a few hours, Elyse a few days. In the late 1940s, neonatal care was primitive and mostly unknown, without the tools to try to save premature babies, particularly at the charity hospital where black babies were born. Husbands were not allowed to be with their wives during delivery.

While Dad was working his shift at Purina Dog Chow in the stockroom, stacking large bags of packaged dog food for store delivery, the foreman came in to congratulate him on the birth of his first baby girl. Dad had taken Mother to the hospital the night before and was told that she could deliver early. No time off was allowed for these paternal events. He left his work number and his foreman's name with the nurses so they could reach him once my mom delivered.

When he heard the news and not knowing much about baby gestational development, he was overjoyed and could hardly wait to finish work so he could get to the hospital and meet his firstborn, a little girl. A few hours later, the foreman came to him again and said, "Green, come on out, we got some bad news. Your baby didn't make it."

Dad said he felt like he'd been punched hard in the stomach and fell to his knees. He immediately left and caught a ride to be with my mother. He held it together until he saw her, and then the young couple wept together, wrapped in each other's arms in the hospital room. They named their baby girl Elaine.

A year or so later, Dad was working at a different job at Allen Woodwork feeding large pieces of wood into a mill. He made $32 a week and after taxes, his pay was $29.20 in cash. Mother was carrying their second child, but she started to experience some pains in her fifth month. News came to him at work that day that his second baby girl, Elyse, had been born. Because she was small, she stayed at the hospital. But she was too young and underdeveloped and she also did not survive. They were deeply heartbroken, but their deep faith helped them continue to believe that God would bless them with a child. Still, they were wary.

My mother conceived again about a year later and carried that baby to six months. He was a beautiful baby boy and the delight of their lives—they named him Green Jr. Though he weighed four pounds, they were allowed to take him home but he developed diarrhea and quickly lost two of those pounds. Dad said, "He looked like a head on a pillow he was so little." Junior, as he was always called, was hospitalized, miraculously survived, and began to thrive.

My parents were so happy to have the blessing of this child. They often dressed him up in handsome clothes, most of which my mother made. As he grew, he learned to scooch around on the floor as my mother kept a spotless house. When Junior was around six months old, my great-grandmother Hattie Osby noticed something while she was visiting; his legs wouldn't stay apart. She urged my mother to get a doctor to check him. She told her in that wise motherly way, "Mae, somethin' wrong with that boy."

They learned that because of his premature birth, there could have been anoxia, a lack of oxygen to the brain. They were told later he was on the cerebral palsy spectrum. My parents did not fully understand, but mother read books so that she could educate herself on this malady, and began to learn what their beloved son would need and how they would provide it. Mother stayed home for a time to care for Junior, but both she and my dad needed to work.

They both brought a deep devotion learned from their families into their own love, and now poured that devotion into the life and well-being of this new baby boy.

As he grew, they learned more about his physical limitations. His particular type, spastic dysplasia, caused muscle stiffness, primarily in the legs. The medical term is hypertonia, 'hyper' meaning high, 'tonia,' pertaining to muscle tone. It presents as stiff and tight leg muscles, creating limited mobility. It described exactly how his legs became as he grew—stiff, with limited mobility.

Junior's legs didn't work for crawling, but this didn't stop him from getting around the house by using his arms to pull the rest of him. Because of this, his upper body became incredibly strong over the years, though his legs and hip joints didn't extend fully. Still, he was a happy, drooling, loving toddler boy, and the old pictures mother kept captured a big smiling wide-eyed little boy looking out from the photos.

Raising Junior was a great joy for my parents, despite his physical challenges. Daddy played on the floor with Junior, gave him piggyback rides and carried him into church. They played catch with him seated, and mother worked with him on speech and diction. They integrated him into every aspect of our lives, and for us, this simply was our family. Junior needed his hand for balancing as he walked the hall of our home, so Dad had wood paneling put on the waist height lower half of the walls where Juniors' big strong hands had worn a dark line. He could easily lose his balance and fall, but his upper body reflexes were so quick that he hardly ever hit the ground. Dad didn't hurry to help him up, but wanted him to help himself. We all watched and learned how to pick ourselves up from his example, learning this self-reliance as he learned it.

I always felt so proud of him even though as a young girl, I didn't understand why his legs didn't work the way ours did. It didn't matter, because it was no big deal. He was our brother, independent and strong. Growing up with this amazing person gave us all a greater sense of empathy and tolerance. He shaped the world as kinder and gentler because of who he was. He could have been labeled "handicapped" by those who didn't know him; fractured in a way the world might see him, but capable and whole in our eyes and in the eyes of God.

Back in the early '50s, the learning curve was great for these childhood illnesses and the repercussions they made on the life of a family. The modalities for surgery and physical therapy were new and developing. We may never know for certain if the cause of Junior's condition was a lack of oxygen to the brain at birth, or some kind of infection. However, his motor cortex, which relays signals to other parts of the brain to control movement, had been damaged.

My parents focused on parenting Junior with inclusivity and a sense of well-being. They raised him as though he had no limits at all. My brother went with us everywhere, and my parents mainstreamed him into public school for many years to foster his sense of normalcy. Despite his limitations, my brother was determined to have a normal life, beyond what society saw for him and closer to the life my parents and he dreamed of.

They searched for ways to help his legs to work so that he could eventually walk. It took several doctor appointments, some good and not-so-good news along the way, and many hospital visits. Twice during his early life, he was given a 50/50 chance of survival, the first when he was a baby and lost two of his four pounds, and the second when he was eight months and became ill and severely dehydrated. After an emergency treatment of intravenous fluid was infused into the only vein they could find on one side of his head, he survived.

Most of the many doctors Junior was taken to were white men, but when he was almost seven, they met a kind female doctor (Daddy called her a "lady doctor"). After assessing my brother, she told them of a special place that she believed could help him walk. It was called Shriners Hospital for Crippled Children. Junior had already under-gone two surgeries in Shreveport to release the quadriceps muscles that were contracted, but those procedures were not as successful as they had hoped. The hospital the doctor suggested was in New Orle-ans, a six-hour car ride from the northwest corner of the boot shaped state where they lived.

Determined, they drove him to Shriners Hospital for a con-sultation. At their visit, they were given the option to stay there for surgery and the physical therapies that followed that would help his labored gait and foster optimal recovery, or they could take him home and let him do the best he could without the specialized therapy at the New Orleans Hospital. It was a huge decision, not only because of the treatment, but because they'd be so far away from him. Mother was overwhelmed, quite anxious, and a bit grieved thinking about how she couldn't fathom leaving him. But they prayed and agreed that they had to do whatever it took to give him the best life possible. They had to find a way.

Each weekend for six months without fail, they made the six-hour one-way drive down two-lane, rural Louisiana roads to see Junior and spend the weekend with him. Sometimes they'd bring along one other traveling friend, and my brother expected them with great anticipation. He, too, felt the distance and longed for their visits. He told me later that he saw children whose parents never visited. He did not want to be one of those kids—it was what he feared the most.

On one of the drives, Dad's water pump blew. He had to go into town to replace the part, which he would discover wasn't available until the next day. Mom and the other lady passenger were left together in the car to wait for his return, with a small revolver for protection. Dad walked a bit toward the next town of Derry, just outside Natchitoches. A kind gentleman and his son picked him up and took him to the nearest car shop. Once there, he learned he couldn't get back to the car where Mother was waiting that evening, because the ride had dropped him off and left. The part would come in the next morning, but there was no way to let mother and her friend know. He prayed they would be safe and protected.

First thing the next morning, Dad bought the car part and got another ride back by the same kind gentleman. He returned to an empty car. He became frantic, worried sick something had happened to these two black women sitting overnight in a car on the side of a highway. He quickly fixed the car's water pump and started driving back to the town, when a state trooper noticed him and turned on his flashing red lights. Now what, Lord?! Dad thought.

The officer walked to the side of the car. "Is your name Green Whitaker?" he asked. Dad was quite surprised that the officer knew his name. "Yes, Officer! I am looking for my wife and her friend. I went to get a part for the car repair and when I—"

The officer interrupted, "Sir, they are waiting for you at the station. We picked them up last night and they're safe."

Dad nearly burst into tears, so relieved that something unkind had not happened to them. "Take me to her!"

He learned that while they waited for him, a trooper had stopped and taken them to the station for the night. Not having any way to communicate with each other was the source of much distress.

When they finally got to the hospital, my brother had been watching out the window for them. He was beside himself with joy, hugs, and tears when they finally arrived, a day late. But they found a way.

This was just one of the adventures on the determined road to see Junior.

After six months of surgeries and physical therapy at Shriners, Junior came home with a metal brace from the waist down. He stood tall with straight legs and braces after his surgery, something they were thrilled about for their son. Once home, he was doing so well that the doctor in town thought they could go with shorter braces from the knee down. Soon after, his legs began to contract and seem to atrophy, his leg posture moving from straight to a thirty-degree bend. He needed to get back to New Orleans for more surgery at Shriners. This time, my mother lived there with him for three months while he was recuperating, with my father driving every weekend to see them. Junior stayed an additional three months, for a total of a year, then was released again.

In Junior's early life, mother read to him and worked diligently with him on speech. He developed good diction and learned to communicate perfectly. He wore a lower body cast and leg braces into his tween years, not walking unassisted until he was thirteen. None of that deterred his will to be accepted for who he was, rather than for how he walked. Many of the other children with intellectual or physical challenges in our community rarely left their houses or the confines of the outer perimeter of their neighborhood, or parents would put them in institutions or group homes if they could not properly care for them. Until Junior could really walk, Daddy would just carry him around on his strong shoulders. As an act of gratitude for helping their son to walk, mother went door to door annually collecting money for Shriner's Hospital March of Dimes charity with me right beside her, collecting dimes for birth defects prevention. As a young child, I remembered that I didn't understand my brother's legs couldn't work the way mine did, but beyond that he was just my brother whom I felt fiercely protective of. As a kid, he played with small yellow Tonka trucks to which he was very attached and had a large collection of them. He loved music too, especially the Motown sounds of Marvin Gaye, Al Green, the Temptations. Junior played his small stereo in his room very loudly and danced until he was sweaty. Dad yelled at him more than once to "turn it down Jr.!" He did, but he kept on playing his music. He was at the age where he developed body odor but he didn't like to bathe. After emerging from a bath not smelling better a few times, Mother peeked through the slightly opened door and saw that he was sitting on the side of the tub fully clothed running his hands through the water, not bathing at all. He got fussed at big time for that. He took real baths after that too.

For most of his life, Junior maintained good close friends in a group of first cousins Ronald Lee and Donald Ray Whitaker, and an older half-brother Scotch Stills who lived a few years with us when he was a teenager. They all watched out for him, fought with him and for him, enjoyed music, laughed hard, and liked a lot of girls together. After high school graduation, Junior was determined not to be a statistic; he did not want to be one of those "crippled" people, as they were called at the time. The job offered and available to him was selling long-life light bulbs in a room with six-foot tables, phones and fluorescent lights, along with others with varying degrees of intellectual or physical disabilities. Junior had decided long before that he didn't belong in that room, and he wanted a regular job working with regular folks.

He found a way. In an act of independence and autonomy, wanting to prove he could get a job on his own, my brother walked ten miles from our home in Cedar Grove to a Travelodge motel near the airport to try to secure a job he had seen advertised. He couldn't afford a bus ticket. Even with the feet-dragging shuffle way he'd learned to walk post braces without a crutch or cane, he made his way on the sidewalks and grassy shoulders to the motel. My brave determined big brother got the job as a part-time dishwasher.

To wash those dishes, he propped himself against the sink's counter for balance. He was so quick and strong with his hands that he ended up doing the work as fast as two people, finding a way to make the job work for him. At seventeen, he was given the weekend shift. Dad drove him to work at 5 a.m. on Saturdays and picked him up at the end of each shift for two consecutive weeks. The employer, seeing how well he worked, hired him full-time, and he started to take the bus to work, even though it still required a few blocks of walking. Because of the way he walked, he wore out the soles of his shoes monthly, so new shoes were regularly required and what a fair part of his pay went toward.

He worked at that hotel for five years until they hired another disabled person, a blind man, to work in the kitchen with him washing dishes. That proved too chaotic and increased his workload because of the extra thing he had to cover for the new employee, so he knew it was time to move on.

Junior walked, eventually rode a bike (though not terribly well), drove a car with specially fitted hand brakes, and had girlfriends—all the small and big things he was told he would not be able to do. Later, he would also become a father, and a grandfather. He never accepted mediocracy, and was exceptional in every way.

After Travelodge, he landed a job at General Electric, where he worked for seven years. He moved from there to General Motors, where he stood on the line making trucks alongside the other workers for another twelve years until the arthritis in his feet became too painful. He made many good friends and memories along the way. Today, he is our family historian and "rolodex", having memorized phone numbers, important events, and birthdays of many of our extended relatives. Along the way, Junior developed the uncanny ability to never take himself too seriously, eager and able to laugh at so much of the silliness he sees in the world and life. He loved working, and would still be working, if the arthritis hadn't stopped him.

Junior's determination for a life closer to what he wanted to be his normal, was in great part because of how mom and dad parented him. They allowed him to believe in himself, and they loved him unconditionally. He wanted what they had, a loving home, a good job, to be seen and accepted, and to have a family—in short, a piece of the American dream. He believed that through hard work, he could achieve his dreams. That love and gentle belief in himself, and his want, drive and determination, spilled over all of us. He wasn't spared spankings when he misbehaved; he was raised just the same as the rest of us. My brother is an outstanding human being and one of the few heroes of my life. He was taught the lessons that my parents lived and showed every day including no matter the challenge, they would always find a way.

They found a way for all of us. In public elementary school, I had many great teachers whose names I can still recall because they loved teaching us so well, and were foundational in my early learning years. I performed in the yearly operettas. Once a week for assembly, I played one of the songs mother taught me to play by ear on the piano, "My Country 'Tis of Thee", with two hands. Mr. Williams, the principal, was a rotund jolly man, as kind as he was round. He wore belted pants high on his wide waist and a suit coat, had the skin the color of coffee with a lot of milk, short-coiled soft black hair with a hairline that was beginning to recede, and a kind face with small brown eyes that twinkled when he smiled. He knew my parents because my mother was the librarian who came to our school on the book mobile, and Dad was a school bus driver for four years.

One time in third grade, I was invited on a class trip to Houston, Texas. I'm not sure why, but I stayed close to Mr. Williams and his wife during that trip. I never heard this story until my late high school days, but sometime after that trip, Mr. Williams came to Dad and asked if they could take me to raise as their own daughter. They did not have children of their own. "Mr. Green, your Nita got under my skin," he told my dad. "My wife and I would like to raise her, give her the best of everything, the best schools and colleges."

My dad paused for a moment to choose his words carefully before he spoke. He wanted to be kind in his response, but knew there was absolutely no way he would ever give his baby girl to anyone else to raise, no matter what they could provide. He said, "Well, Nita is a special sweet child, and that is very flattering and kind, but we gon' find a way to give her everything that she needs."

Just as he and Mother found a way to give my brother the best start to his life, they did that for me as well. From summer Christian camps and a theater camp for me, summer family trips, musical instrument lessons, going to see college Shakespeare plays, they endeavored to show us the big world beyond our neighborhood. I once heard that when you witness better you often want better.

The example of courage from my brother and the inspiration from my father and mother were transformational examples for me. Those three words — "find a way" — are a resilient reminder that we all must find a way: to be, to do, to reach our goals and dreams. And when obstacles come my way, and they do come, I hear my dad say, "Find a way, Nita."

That's what keeps me going.

*Me and my brother
Green Jr.*

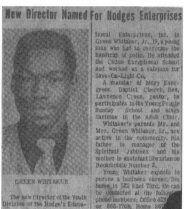

*My brother Green Whitaker Jr.
(correction, he did not have polio...)*

*Jr. dressed up next to his car in our
neighborhood, Cedar Grove"*

*Principle Williams
at Stoner Hill Elementary School*

Our parents Green and Ola Mae Whitaker at daughter Alene's wedding

CHAPTER 16

A Good Name Is Better Than Silver Or Gold

Of the five part-time jobs my dad worked, two were in the homes of the two wealthy families of Dr. John Atkins and his sister, Caroline Crawford. Dad met these siblings through a friend who recommended him, and who also worked for them. Word of my dad's beautiful lawn manicuring skills and his natural "green" thumb resulted in the doctor and his sister hiring him to take care of their yards once a week.

Because of Dad's impeccable work in his own yard, it was once photographed by the local paper and named the "Best Lawn in Cedar Grove." He applied those same skills to care for their yards. He would later be rewarded with bonus pay and compliments, as well as establishing so much trust that he was eventually asked to oversee their expansive homes when they traveled. He took care of the exterior grounds and occasionally waxed the floors of their den along with cleaning the entry chandelier.

He had only been working for Mrs. Crawford for a month or so when she seemed to set a trap for him. Perhaps she needed to know that she could trust him with so much going on in her home. She asked him to clean her upstairs bathroom, just off her master bedroom, while she went out to play bridge. This wasn't a typical request. He began to begin to clean as instructed, but immediately noticed she'd left her large diamond ring in the bathroom. His first instinct upon seeing it on the counter, he told me, was that it shouldn't be left out like that because it could be stolen. His second thought? Perhaps she was testing his integrity and left it out on purpose. So he took the sizable ring and placed it in the top drawer in the bathroom so it would be out of sight. He then cleaned and polished the marble floor there as she had requested.

When Mrs. Crawford returned from her outing, she hurried

upstairs. Dad was downstairs taking his usual care of their den, and noticed the way her eyes darted at him before dashing up the stairs. After a few minutes up there, Dad heard her shuffling around in the bedroom for a few minutes. Dad called out, "Ahhh, excuse me, Mrs. Crawford, look there in the top drawer in the bathroom there, ma'am. You left your ring out and I put it there in for safe keeping." In that moment, she knew the character of the man came through in word and deed.

Upon hearing this, she stepped slightly out of her bedroom door to acknowledge him as Dad addressed her from the bottom of the stairs. "I don't steal, Mrs. Crawford. I come here and do my work and get out. If I want something here, I'll ask you. But I wouldn't take nothin' from you. Ever."

She smiled, nodded briefly, and retreated in her floral fit-and-flare dress.

From that moment on, he became a treasured employee. Mrs. Crawford's young daughter became so enchanted with my dad that she wouldn't eat her lunch unless she could sit with him when he was there. This was during the mid 60s, when the lion of segregation divided blacks and whites separating them especially at dining tables. Dad, being Dad, was the exception in this home. Mrs. Crawford would have their maid make him homemade lunches when he worked so he could eat them with their daughter in the kitchen. He became indispensable to their families and worked for them for five years.

Dad noticed bags of clothes at their door one day, on their way to a charity, and asked if he could buy some things from it for his girls. "Just take it, Green," Dr. Atkins said. After that, Dr. Atkins would send us girls expensive hand-me-downs that his daughters had outgrown, things like tailored English coats, pastel smock dresses, and expensive leather boots and purses.

We reaped the benefit of these amazing clothes. People in our black neighborhood assumed, because we were well-dressed and well shod kids, that our family had money. In truth, it was our dad's good name that brought us those beautiful garments. The trust he earned, his openness, integrity and innate kindness gave him a reputation as an honorable man within the local society of wealthy people.

Daddy's desire to provide a good life for his family began with his tenacious work ethic and pride in his work. He told us that he never "wanted something he didn't work for," and planted the seeds of his appreciation of work many times in us by saying, "If you want something, get a job and work for it. If you want more, get another or a better job to get what you want." Mom and Dad would say often, "A good name is better than silver or gold," based on a scripture from Proverbs that states, "A good reputation is more desirable than great wealth and favorable acceptance more than silver and gold."

I heard that a lot growing up, but as I matured, the meaning of that scripture became clearer. A good name, or reputation, can be your passport to getting more in your life. It can open doors that nothing else can. Dad taught us to mind our characters and the choices we made, even while young, so that we could build on our own good names.

Dr. Atkins told my dad at one point that he trusted him more than his own brother. Not only did Dad do a consistently great job caring for their lawns, but wherever he worked, he did so with great pride and always to the best of his ability. Dad's honorable behavior, personal moral courage was rewarded with favorable recommendations and financial bonuses. This added to his life's worth. He became known not only by his unusual name, but the quality of person he was in all aspects of his life. This may not be the path for everyone whose personality isn't like his, but I believe he was hardwired that way, and truly and still is, a lover of all people.

My parents weren't people of great financial wealth, by any stretch of the imagination. But there was worth in their word, and wealth in their faith and love of family. They were simply two people who shared a world view to lead with love and excellence, do good wherever they could, and to be honorable in all things. They bred that into us, not by will or by force, but by example. Because they unknowingly understood that children imitate behavior, they showed behavior they wanted us to imitate.

CHAPTER 17
Don't Always Hurry To A Green Light

For most of my growing up years, my dad drove a school bus. It was his steady bread and butter income, one in which he took great pride. He also won many awards for safe driving over the years from the school board and was beloved by the community of children he carried. This afforded him an opportunity not only to drive his children to and from school, but to hear the conversations of our peers and other children in the community.

The bright yellow bus was a long tunnel with thirteen rows of dark brown colored leatherette seats on either side with a black metal bar structure attached to its back, which made a four- legged support underneath its bench. Its floor was covered with a thin black rubberized material that prevented slips from wet shoes on rainy days. The side windows could slide halfway down by squeezing two tabs, and there were double doors at the back for emergency exit. There were no seat belts.

For the first four years of my elementary school, Dad drove me and my sisters to our respective schools across town. We loved being on Dad's bus for our rides to and from school. After he'd drop all the other children off, he'd drive down Gilbert street, a wide two lane street that had three hills with beautifully recessed homes with manicured lawns on either side. Daddy knew just how to drive over the crests of those hills, so that we'd get butterflies time and time again. Some years later, he drove my brother on a bus specially equipped with a wheelchair lift to pick up other students all headed to the High School for Exceptional Children, as it was called, with other special needs children. Dad learned many safety strategies while driving for so many years, and was always our careful defensive driver on family car trips, to and from church on Sundays, or wherever we went.

His long yellow bus was parked across the street diagonally from our home in a huge square, partially grassy lot that had once been the turnaround termination point for the city bus; it was as far south as the bus would pick up passengers. Later, it became the lot for three school buses, but after a couple of vandal attacks, dad extended our driveway and parked the bus close to our home for the last years that he was a driver. Some days, my cousin Debbie and I would open the doors and play a game, "Guess Where I'm Going". Careful not to touch the gas pedal or gear shift, we would call out turns, right or left, and street names, to see if the other could figure out where we ended up by our driving descriptions and what we'd passed by.

On a routine morning, we boarded the bus and headed out to pick up the other children. We started on the narrow four-lane main city street, Line Avenue, that ran the north and south length through town. After he pulled onto it from 73rd Street, the first traffic signal was at 70th Street. Alene sat across the aisle from us and my sister Kathy and I sat directly behind Dad, with a metal l-shaped bar between us.

This morning, I noticed something was different. Dad's big Whitaker ears turned dark red and seemed to stick out even more than usual as we approached the light. "Hold on chil'ren!" he yelled as he moved the gear shift with some urgency. Without slowing down, he swerved the bus through a corner gas station and I then saw water shooting up into the air as we passed a row of gas pumps. He took another quick jerky right as I held onto that pole in front of me for dear life. Daddy said no other words, but I could tell from his body that he was focused as he wielded the long yellow bus. He managed to weave the bus, somehow narrowly missing another row of gasoline pumps. He took one more sharp left onto 70th Street, where the bus came to a slow roll and stopped. It felt like forever in slow motion, though it was probably only a few minutes that we tossed and swerved in that bus with dad masterfully maneuvering.

The owner of the neighborhood store just across the street, Mr. Bolton, rushed out to assist us. My big sister Alene yanked the lever to open the bus doors and took off running the three blocks for home to alert our mother, who was still there getting ready for her library job that started at 9 AM. My little skinny legs were barely able to hold my weight as I tried to stand. The adrenaline rushed in, causing my whole body to tremble from all the fright and erratic movement that had tossed my seven-year-old body like a windy flag waving high on a pole.

I later learned that the bus's brakes had failed, though they had been serviced the day before. My dad would have hit about six waiting cars full of parents and children at the light if he had not avoided them by his smart maneuvering through the gas station, which ultimately slowed the bus to a stop. When he went to brake, the pedal went to the floor; in that split second, instead of pulling the emergency brake, which could have thrown us forward and through the windows, and still not allowed enough time to stop the bus before plowing into those waiting cars, he chose to slow the bus by weaving and avoid harming people with the 10,000-pound vehicle.

"You girls alright?" he asked as he stood, pulling the emergency brake, himself shaking. He helped me and my sister Kathy off the bus. When I got to the bottom step, my legs gave way, I collapsed, and the tears flowed. He scooped me up, gently hugged me and kissed my cheek, and reminded me that we were all okay. Mr. Bolton brought me a coke in a small glass bottle to calm and console me, which I began to sip as Dad went to survey the damage to the station and the bus. He and the other people in some of the cars pulled over to see if we were okay. Mr. Bolton and others told my dad after they learned his brakes had failed, they were amazed at his driving skills and how he maneuvered the hulking yellow school bus, saving not only his daughters and the occupants in the cars, but also managed to avoid any major property damage.

He was already my hero, but that day, he became my superhero.

Dad would always give little tidbits of driving knowledge when we were in the car. He'd plant safety tips long before we were driving on our own, things like, "You have to watch out for the other drivers." And I noticed one day that he'd slowed down a bit when approaching an intersection with a green light for his lane. I said, "Dad, why are you slowing down? The light is green."

"Don't always hurry to a green light," he cautioned us.

At first, it didn't make sense. Most of us think that if you see a green light, that means go, so you speed up to get through the light. But Dad cautioned against that. He told me, "You have to look around to see what other cars are doing; sometimes, people make a right turn, and if you are rushing to get through that green light, that's when accidents can happen."

I came to realized that don't always hurry to a green light is also be a metaphor for how to move and choose in life. Hurrying to a green light means that just because you can do a thing doesn't mean you should. Hurrying to a green light is when the door is wide open, but you know you shouldn't go in. Hurrying to a green light can mean taking the easier shortcut or cheating when there is an honest, more deliberate path to your goals. Hurrying to a green light is doing all the things you want to do and not so much of the things you should do. Green lights are a good thing; they keep us going forward, but we must remember not to rush through.

Not hurrying to a green light is slowing down to take in the landscape of what is happening in that moment, to do what's right even if is not easy, and moving through with caution and clarity. So even now, as my adult daughter tells me to "Hurry up, Mom, the light is green," I return the gem to her as it was given to me, and caution her as my father did me in the hope she, with time, can metaphorically understands that green lights are great when we get them or give them to ourselves in life. Either way, proceed with caution and optimism.

CHAPTER 18

People Are Just People

———◆———

"Daddy, are all white people rich?"

He thought for a moment before answering me. "People are just people. We all the same, just come here in different skins."

The only white people we knew growing up were the wealthy ones my dad worked for, who were more than generous with their expensive hand-me-downs and lived in enormous homes with big white antebellum columns in the front. I thought that's how all white people lived. Our elementary school, Stoner Hill, was predominately black, our rural church congregation was all black, and our neighbors were, too. My world was colorful and filled with the most beautiful shades of brown people.

"Come on, let's take a ride, Nita," he said, leading me and one of my siblings to the 1964 beige Pontiac sedan we owned. He drove us to an area of town I didn't know existed. Dad drove us to a particular area of town, where we saw white people sitting on porches of houses in disrepair, shelling peas and waving to passersby. Non-running cars and trucks were propped up on cinder blocks, rusted from oxidation and lack of use. There were sparse lawns of mostly dirt with some patches of grass here and there. Dirt-smeared little white children were running around in worn clothes in those yards, dogs lapping at their heels as they played and giggled, aproned mothers in curtain-less kitchen windows washing dishes or making meals. Some houses were well kept and others in need of repairs and paint. Their neighborhood looked like parts of ours. As we drove slowly down the street, I noticed the people living there were doing the same things we did. I clearly remember snapping that image in my mind of ordinary people doing ordinary things in ordinary houses. They were just like us, but in a different skin.

Dad had witnessed it in the wealthy families he worked for; that they had the same issues, concerns and troubles like people with less wealth. Theirs just cost more.

Dad had a white coworker who made some wooden benches that were also toy storage for the girls' bedroom. He brought them over to the house one day and sat for a short chat and dessert after he and dad installed them. Some neighbors commented that we had "white folk visiting at our house." Dad said, "he was just a friend from work who made furniture and so what if he was white? He's a man just like me."

In fifth grade, we were told I had to go to the school in our neighborhood, called Atkins Elementary. I didn't know at the time that it was because of desegregation laws. Had I known, I may not have grasped the concept even if explained. My parents kept it simple to say that I was going to make some new friends at a new school. I wondered why the new friends didn't come to my old school and instead of my dad being my bus driver now, I'd walk to the end of my block and a bus with other elementary aged kids from my neighborhood, would pick me up and drop me back there after school. For the second half of that school year, I moved to another predominantly black school called 81st Street elementary. I am not sure why, but remembered our Pastor Clarence Williams and his family lived in one of the houses across the street from the school. One day, the strap broke on the shoes I was wearing and caused them to flop when I walked. I was so embarrassed and went to the office to call home. Thank goodness my dad was there and when I heard his voice, I began to cry. I was not a big crier so he knew that I was upset. Within a half hour, my handsome dad came to the school and appeared in the door of my classroom. All 6'2 1/2" with his wavy black hair slicked back with Murrays, wearing a short-sleeved shirt with pocketed front and belted pleated pants, he looked so dashing. He scooped me up, gave me a hug, then knelt to sit me on one knee just outside the classroom where he placed another pair of shoes from home on my feet. Then gave me a big hug and a cheek kiss before he strode away, back to his next job. Daddy made me feel so special in that moment. I had never seen anyone's dad come to school before to bring their embarrassed daughter a pair of shoes, and neither had they. For weeks after, the small school was abuzz with talk of the kind handsome father who brought shoes for his little girl.

So when I walked into my new Atkins Elementary School for the first day of fifth grade, and the classroom was dotted with gentle peach faces with blond or brunette hair, I took my seat among them across from my cousin Debbie. It didn't feel extraordinary to me, maybe because there were also a few brown faces there too, but I also knew I could learn and was a good student and the peach children didn't seem threatened by our being there. I already felt special before I got there. However, I am quite aware that wasn't every little black girls' experience in our history of school integration. I missed seeing the beautiful brown faces of my teachers at Stoner Hill Elementary and 81st Street school, and all my friends there. Because I remembered what my dad told me and showed me—that we are just people in different skins, making new friends came easily. After all, people are just people.

Dad and me at a church picnic

CHAPTER 19
Close Yo' Door

One of the unspoken rules in my childhood home was that bedroom doors were always left open. It wasn't something that was announced, it just was. Our home grew to become a three-bedroom, two-bath house, enlarging as our family did. Interestingly, our door was also open to family and friends; all were welcome.

Several of my younger aunts (mom's sisters) stayed with us through their high school and college years, cousins and uncles dropped by when our parents were home, mission meetings were held in our home, and out-of-town family guests often stayed with us. I always felt rich because of the life inside that sweet home on 73rd Street. I was raised with fruit trees in the back yard and a happy protective dog named Skinny. Dad meticulously manicured our front and back lawns every week. Our Jetson's-themed remodeled kitchen had shiny white formica countertops with orange high-backed swivel leatherette chairs that had white tulip bases and the solid white round pedestal table at its center was way ahead of its time for our neighborhood. Mother always kept some sweet cakes under glass and I was so proud of what I thought of as our "mini-mansion" because my parents had not only worked hard but they worked smart.

A local paper interviewed me at our home after I won the Miss Shreveport pageant, the first woman of color to do so. The reporter started his article by saying he'd visited me in my "modest home." Modest? I was mildly offended. I always thought our home was grand.

I learned recently that we were called the "Black Kennedys of Cedar Grove"—the name of our subdivision in Shreveport where cedar trees had once grown. And occasionally I'd hear, "Y'all daddy trying to raise y'all like white girls." The words carried no weight with me then or now, because our parents always taught us that we were no better or worse than any other.

We went on family vacations almost every summer, even if it was just a drive in the family Pontiac to Dallas. When staying at a Holiday Inn or eating at a Howard Johnson's, I'd always ask when we traveled, "Daddy, where are the brown people?" He'd just say, "Oh, they are doing other things or relaxing at home." The passing world from the front seat of our Pontiac was so exciting and it opened the door to what the world looked like beyond my town, church, and community. We had two working cars in the carport and two parents who worked full-time jobs while nurturing our family. It was unusual for people in our neighborhood to own more than one car. My parents never commented on what people said, but simply worked for their share of the dream in America, lived their lives and tried to give us more than they'd been afforded or was even possible for them. They gave their four children a life with as many open doors as they could find for us.

Yes there were rules and boundaries, home-cooked meals, and figuring out how to get along with each other, but mostly unconditional love and acceptance from the two at the helm. They allowed us to find our way and to just be kids. There was so much magic in them because they openly adored each other and we watched and learned. My parents also celebrated our individual uniqueness, created holiday traditions and summer travel, and gave us the freedom to run and play with abandon. They allowed us to be silly kids turning cartwheels in the front yard, or playing ball in the streets with our neighbors. They created a home where music and giggles were allowed—and mistakes were, too—and where make-believe was not made fun of. They showed us their love and loving ways in countless hugs and kisses, giving us a home that grew within us a sense of wellbeing, no matter what was going on outside our doors. A home like this was the best gift a parent could ever give to their child.

Another door they opened for us led into the world of music. Music was an essential part of our lives since Dad was a soloist, group, and choir singer. Mother also sang in the choir, and we all sang in the youth choirs at church and school. Music ran through the veins of our family and coursed through the halls of our home. We had an upright not well tuned piano in our living room, and all us girls took piano lessons with a neighborhood teacher. We played other instruments through our public school band and orchestra programs. I picked up the violin in fourth grade and could also play piano by ear. When I was learning to play the violin, screeching sounded from the haired bow sawing across the metal strings as I tried to place my fingers correctly for "Twinkle Twinkle Little Star". I used to get inspiration for a song and run to the piano at midnight or 1:00 a.m. to play out the melody and lyric ideas in my head. The sound would waft up the hall and drive my sister, Kathy, crazy. "Daddy! Tell Nita to stop making that noise!"

"Close yo' door!" Dad would shout back to her.

That one closed door allowed an open window for creativity to flourish from its infancy within me. I love that he recognized that in me and allowed it to grow and bloom. Having that kind of support gave me the foundation to pursue an artistic career. I was allowed to be a breaking-into-songs, screeching violin playing, song-writing-in-the-middle-of-the-night- Nita.

The piano in the Living Room on 73rd Street

CHAPTER 20

Nothin' Open After 11 But Legs

When we were in elementary school, we were only allowed to play in the backyard or on the dusty gravel road in front of our house with neighborhood friends Steve and Ricky Combs, Mary Sue First (I always loved her three names), Quinton and Phillip, Darryl and Ulette. Our weekends were consumed by choir rehearsals, house cleaning chores, and church. We went inside for homework and dinner by dusk, and maybe some television. No visitors were allowed when our parents weren't home, not even relatives.

Green Whitaker's girls weren't allowed to officially date until they were sixteen. (I didn't really have a date at sixteen, but because my cousin Jerry Adams didn't have anyone to go with, I was asked to his prom.) That did not mean we didn't notice a boy or two – or they noticed us – but it was just that, a look now and then. My father laid down strict rules. One of them was our curfew.

My parents created safety checks so that they had a handle on where we were most times. They worked as a team. We had to get both parents' permission to visit anyone, even relatives. We had to let one of them know when we were leaving, and call when we arrived at our destination. We asked one parent and then the other, and if we used the words, "Can I?" my mother would reply with, "I don't know if you can or not." We had to start with "May I?" They didn't make it easy for us to go anywhere and my mother was a stickler for proper language and good diction.

I wondered why it was all so necessary, but once I became a mother, I understood. Even though Dad was a marshmallow inside, he and Mother figured out ways to keep us a bit safer by implementing these rules so they would clearly know where we were going and with whom. Dad would mostly be the one to deliver the final verdict.

Big hugs and cheek kisses were just as plentiful as the rules in our house. The strict rules and standards gave us hard boundaries. As we grew and wanted to stretch our wings, there was a tethering that felt unfair at the time, especially when we would see some of our friends enjoying the freedoms we wanted so badly. Dad softened a bit on some rules as we got older, like not wearing shorts on Sundays, or getting spared the spanking my older siblings Alene and Jr. got.

I was very clear with my dad at five years old after seeing my brother get a spanking across his knee, that I never wanted him to do that to me. I told him, "You just tell me what you don't want me to do and I won't do it." We kept that pact.

Now I was hoping I could get them to lighten some of the hard lines on my curfew. I was the last one home, other than my brother who was working full time. Because he was a working adult, he was subject to different rules. My best friend and cousin Debbie's curfew was at midnight, and I was hoping to sway Dad so that mine could be, too. I was a hard-working student and an overall good kid; I loved learning and had worked for my good grades.

First, I tried it out on my mom, even though no matter how many times I asked her she would always say, "You have to ask Daddy to see what he thinks about that." I asked her if she thought Dad would let me have a later curfew, hoping her affirmative response would get Dad to change his mind. No such luck.

So I got up the nerve. It was one day in the eleventh grade, after Debbie asked me about going to a house party around the corner from my house. I asked Dad if I could go and stay out until twelve, like most other kids. "Daddy, could I have my curfew extended to midnight?" I asked him earnestly, thinking since I had been such an obedient girl, and never any trouble, that I had earned the right.

"No, you can't," he said, without looking up from his bedroom desk.

"But all my friends have curfews at midnight, and it seems like they are all okay—"

"The answer is still no, Nita," he interrupted.

"I just don't understand. Can you tell me why it can't be midnight like everybody else? I'm responsible," I persisted.

He finally stopped what he was doing and looked at me. Without raising his voice and barely raising an eyebrow, he said, "Ain't nothin' open after eleven but legs. So be home by eleven."

"Yes sir, Daddy."

I tucked my tail and went to my room.

Later, I went to the party, but checked my watch frequently. I made sure I was walking out the door at 10:45 and that my behind was home for my 11 o'clock curfew.

CHAPTER 21
You Think Money Grows On Trees?

I've heard the saying "being born on third base or born with a silver spoon", both meaning there was an advantage by being born into affluence and other privileges. My family was certainly not one with financial wealth, a surname that could open a door into the wider world or help me get into social circles or the right university. What we were given, though, was a sense of frugality and the value of a hard-earned dollar.

My parents' simplicity was their strength. Their common sense was their loaded bank account, and their raw intelligence was a gift that helped our family grow. What our parents taught us was a product of what they had learned in the farming life, though they both worked to make a better life for our entire family than the one into which they had been born. The life they exemplified, the pearls of thoughts, wisdom, and goodness gave us an early entry to the school of life, a work ethic, and a leg up in the game of common sense.

As children, we had to ask our parents for money if we wanted something outside of our basic needs. When I was in elementary school and junior high, a quarter could buy so many treats at Ms. Bee's store on Line Avenue. Ten cents bought five big cookies, stored in several large clear containers with a lid. They had a large jar of pickled pigs' feet, Bit-O-Honey, Sugar Babies, Chick- O-stick candies, and many other goodies at the counter, along a deli counter at the back of the store where they would slice meats and cheese. If we needed something quick and did not want to go to the big A&P grocery store, we would instead take a three-minute walk from our house to this small local grocery store, owned by two black women who were sisters.

We weren't given allowances, but we all had chores. The bi-yearly spring and fall cleaning meant taking everything out of each cupboard, drawer, and closet, wiping everything down, cleaning, purging, and restoring. Our kitchen and floor cleaning duties rotated weekly but we all learned how to clean a house, wash and iron our clothes, make beds and dust the house. Until we held our own small paying jobs, we would ask our parents for what we wanted or needed.

My first paying job came when I was ten, playing piano for the junior choir at our church every fourth Sunday. They paid me eight dollars. I thought I was rolling in the dough. My parents then took me to the local First National Bank to start my first savings account. It was such a thrill to go in monthly with my little savings card and watch it start to grow.

But before this time of earning, I had a way of asking for a dollar from my daddy. Here was the scenario: "Daddy, can I have a dollar?"

"I don't know if you can or not," he'd reply.

"*May* I have a dollar?"

"Whatcha need a dollar for?" he'd say.

"I want to get some toiletries and things at the five and dime store."

Then he'd call my mother and involve her. "Mae, Nita saying she needs a dollar. Whatcha think about it?" It felt like a game of cat and mouse sometimes, but they wanted to be sure that I understood what I was asking for.

"Mom, I just want to get some new perfume to smell nice and some treats at TG &Y, the five-and-dime store," I'd say, nearing exasperation and bordering on embarrassment for even asking.

He'd then look directly at me. "You think money grows on trees?"

"No, sir, I don't. That's okay, just forget about it. I don't need it." I withdrew and started to walk away.

Then, with one swift move at the eleventh hour, he'd pull one single dollar from some folded bills deep in his front pocket. And then he'd say, "Now you bring me back some change."

When I was fourteen, my favorite cousin Booker T. (we called him Red) hired me and my cousin Debbie to work at his tailoring shop in the summer. He paid us each fourteen dollars a week to assist him in taking measurements of the clients that came in for custom-made clothing and alterations. That was a lot of money! Red had instructed us never to measure men's inseam and I knew why. Many of the clients were women but there were also a lot of men. Once in a while he would leave us alone in the store with a client or while he ran an errand. I was always keenly aware that we were two fourteen-year-old girls alone in a storefront, but we did not feel afraid. It gave us a sense of empowerment and independence that he trusted us to run his small shop.

My dad made sure I saved at least ten dollars from it, each and every week. My favorite treat was to get a hamburger with a coke at Mr. Swiss, a burger chain, then go to the five and dime store for some girly things like lacy socks, a new coin purse, hair accessories, or some new pens or pencils. It was my first work experience outside of church. This job taught me the value in work, of showing up every day ready to do my best, of earning a dollar and saving. My attitude about money today stems from those back-and-forth exchanges with my parents, and watching how Dad masterfully stretched a dollar while raising the four of us who wanted so much. And we had a good life in Cedar Grove.

As a boy, Dad earned only a dollar a day for twelve hours in the field. I was taught not to take money for granted, and that it certainly didn't grow on trees.

CHAPTER 22

Ain't Nothin' Better Than Water

One of the summer destinations our parents used to take us to was Hot Springs, Arkansas. Dad had heard from some folks at his work that there was hot mineral water there bubbling up from deep wells in the earth, and it was the "fountain of youth" elixir. He longed for the taste of the well water on which he had grown up, and he used this first trip to see if what they were talking about was true. He was always a lover of the taste of water, as he found nothing better quenched his thirst after a long hard day of work. Until he was nearly grown, water was their most plentiful drink, not soda pop. A treat would be "sugar water", water with a stirred spoonful of sugar.

The drive took three hours with my mother and the four of us in tow. Since I was the smallest, I usually sat in the front seat between my parents, though sometimes I would switch with my sister Kathy. It was also for comfort's sake that we rode that way because we were the smallest. I loved our car trips which was the only way we could afford to travel, and I loved the middle front seat view. I could see the whole sky and open road with no visor blocking the expansive display. The clouds danced and played with me on every journey as I watched how they shape-shifted and changed form.

On longer trips, before my legs got too long, the space between the car's back window and back seat was roomy enough for me to crawl in and take a horizontal nap. We snacked on mother's home-made fried bologna sandwiches with mayonnaise and skillet toast white Wonder Bread, fried pork chop sandwiches, chicken, Lay's potato chips, Hostess Cupcakes and Twinkies that mom bought at our local Wonder Bread thrift store, along with some cold pop and water kept in a cooler in the large roomy trunk.

I always had lots of questions as we drove through the small towns of any road trip, because I wanted to know everything. My daddy always gave answers, followed by more questions from me. Sometimes we'd sing on the ride, joining in together, or Dad would play gospel music, some Mahalia Jackson, the Mighty Clouds of Joy or the Alabama Blind Boys on the 8-track player in our four-door 1964 beige Pontiac Bonneville. Sometimes, there'd be silence.

When I was about twelve, Dad bought his first Cadillac (white with a navy top and interior). It doubled as both our family car and one of the cars used to drive families during funerals on weekends when he started his part ownership in Good Samaritan Funeral home in Shreveport. Still he let us drive that beautiful car because he said, it was just a car. He always said the we were more important than any "thing". And later when I heard that song from *Dreamgirls* about the Cadillac car, Dad owning one had a whole new meaning. Until then, he kept the Bonneville in immaculate shape, wiping it down every morning at home and keeping up on the maintenance and changing the oil himself. We all learned to drive in that Bonneville so in a way it had a feeling of home.

Each trip was an adventure into the wider world. It was incredibly interesting to me that we saw few people that looked like our family when we traveled, but I enjoyed each car adventure and destination we went in that big comfy car.

Mother read and researched things to do and places to go before we went anywhere, being a librarian. She was always eager for us to learn and see something new. Even though that trip to Arkansas was a mini-vacation, Daddy was also eager to find this precious mineral water, and Mother learned there was an IQ Zoo museum. We went there that first time — and each time afterward, it was where we all wanted to go again.

After Dad paid the admission fee, we walked inside the blond brick two-story building, dark grey industrial carpet beneath our feet. Once inside, there was a large open room lit with dim ceiling pin lights that shined on several glass enclosures. In those enclosures were chickens, rabbits, a goose, and other barn animals that could all do some tricks. A token or coin was required in the slot below their glass, and then a brighter light would turn on as the animal performed the trained trick, which I found fascinating. One could play a tiny piano, while another dunked a small basketball. One would hit a ball holding a bat in its beak and run around a small baseball diamond. Long before I learned about Pavlov's dog in my nursing training or had a sense of animal welfare, I couldn't fathom how they trained these animals to do tricks when I couldn't get my dog to respond to "sit" and "stay".

When we got to the fillin' station (that's what we called gas stations), Dad asked someone how to get to the place where the water was. As we drove through the town of Hot Springs, we would see signs that said "BATHS." I asked what that was since the only baths we knew were in our home tubs. Mom said, "People come here from all over to bathe in the hot mineral water. It comes up from the earth hot and it is supposed to be good for aches and pains."

But Dad was headed to the place up a mountainous road to get some of this water he could take back. He was always watching out for the other drivers, because he knew accidents happened when somebody wasn't looking. He also had a fear of heights. As we climbed higher on the road, he asked us to be quiet, no music and no talking; he didn't want any distraction on the curvy mountainous road. Soon, there we were: a landing up high with a view, where people brought empty jugs to a row of spigots and filled them with this water. Daddy filled one just a little and took a large gulp; he declared it "mighty good water!" He only brought ten empty plastic milk jugs, but filled them all. And it was free.

Maybe it was the fountain of youth, or maybe he was teaching us the importance of drinking water long before it was smart and cool or nutritionally sound. When he came in from mowing the lawn or from working outdoors and after chugging a tall glass full, he'd often say, "Chil'ren, ain't nothing better than water but more water!" He encouraged all of us to drink more.

Seeing how beautifully he has aged, along with never developing a taste for alcohol, his secret is out: it's all about the water. Scientists, dietitians, and nutritionists now emphasize what my dad has been saying and doing all along.

At ninety-six, he has been graced with the gift of gentle aging; most think he is 20 years younger, but I know his secret. To this day, my dad makes a couple trips yearly to Hot Springs to replenish his supply. He still drinks about a gallon of water a day. And still, after a meal or just in general, he'll swig down a big glass of that cool water, finish with a big "Ah!" and say, "Chil'ren! I keep telling you, ain't nothin' better than water but MORE water!"

Family vacation in Hot Springs, Arkansas
Jr., Alene, Mom, me, and Kathy

Hot Springs with Daddy.
From left to right, Alene, Dad, Me, and Kathy

CHAPTER 23
Go All The Way

I loved to watch my daddy shave his face when I was a little girl. It was part of his morning routine, one that is still a part of his day.

He'd fill the sink with warm water, soap up his face (sometimes he'd use shaving cream if he had it) and began his meticulous clean shave, leaving only his black mustache. A sweep across the right cheek, then another, until all the white was gone, pausing only to wash the razor in the warm water and repeat. He looked into the mirror as he went along, and then down when he rinsed. Sometimes, Daddy would hand me the razor and let me pull it across his face, making little roads of shiny brown skin that contrasted with the white soapy foam. I'd giggle, thinking that was the coolest thing ever.

Our family home had two bathrooms, both with double sinks and a mirror that extended between them. We called the one nearest the living/dining room the "front" bathroom, the other we called "Mommy and Daddy's" because it was newer and closest to their bedroom. I would sit on the counter between the sinks, usually on a weekend, and we'd have little chats there, beginning when I was in elementary school.

In my first semester at NLU, now called ULM, our mother died and my dad was left with the task of continuing to parent us and keep us a family, which he did. We were all adjusting to the huge loss of our sweet Mother. We didn't understand how sick she was with kidney disease, though she'd been hospitalized multiple times. Because of her young age of forty-nine, we thought she would surely survive. Mom had been ahead of her time; as a conservationist advocate and as a public school book mobile librarian, she had a heart for children. She was head of the youth department at our church (picking up the neighborhood kids and bringing them to church weekly) and led the Vacation Bible School camp each summer. But disease knows no name, face, or kindness; it just happens sometimes to the very best people. She was much beloved in our community and church, and her death had a huge ripple effect across our village that included her mother and thirteen living siblings. For everyone who knew her, worked with her, and for the children across the city and rural communities she served who lovingly called her "the book lady" on the bookmobile, there was a sense of great loss. Her services were attended by so many that the overflow crowd outside the church was more than those within. The funeral procession to her resting place at Good Hope Presbyterian church was more than a mile long. More than our family knew and felt we'd lost a treasure.

My awesome Mother was a great cook, mentor to her thirteen younger siblings, and knew how to laugh and be downright silly. She loved to dress for work and loved beautiful sleeping gowns for nighttime. The loss of our mother was a huge blow to the fabric and foundation of our entire family. We all tried to figure out how to move through the grief that was both terrifically sad and unbelievable.

Occasionally, I'd come home from college on weekends to play for a church, which gave me some additional needed income, but the smells and memories of mother lingered, constant reminders that she was not with us. I heard my dad crying late at night and felt helpless. I realized that I had no idea how to express my grief over this enormous loss. But I remembered her belief that I could become anything I wanted if I worked for it, and I tried to focus on that and make her and Dad proud of me.

My eldest sister, Alene, married at nineteen, while mother was still with us. However, my middle sister Kathy's grief proved too great; she left college, helped Dad with his debit insurance work, and later became a mother to our first nephew. My brother Jr. poured his sadness into focused work at General Electric. A few weeks after mother died, Jr. fell asleep at the wheel, somehow missing a head-on collision but totaling the car. He walked away unscathed and shared that later that same night, mother came to him; he saw her, he said, "as plain as day". She wanted us to carry on, keep going and I knew how important our education was to her and my dad, so I wanted to not only continue, but make them both proud, and be able to help Dad with his expenses.

I had always been a driven student, an overachiever, thinking at one time that I'd like to go to medical school. Also, I knew that medical school would be cost-prohibitive for my widowed Dad. Instead, I could get through the four-year nursing program and help my dad pay the outstanding medical bills from Mother's illness. With a love for math and science, a curiosity about how things work, and a nurturing nature, I resolved that becoming a registered nurse would be close enough, because I would work right alongside the doctors.

Late in my second semester of college, my father said some of the most profound words ever to me. On Saturday, during one of my weekends home, I passed by the bathroom and noticed he had begun his daily shave. I plopped my lanky body on the white Formica counter between the two green sinks and we began a chat. He asked me how school was going and about my classes and new friends. Once, while he was rinsing the razor, Dad looked away from the mirror and up at me and said simply, "Nita, I'mma need you to go all the way."

"Yes sir, Daddy, that's my plan," I said.

He didn't expound, didn't add anything more, just went right back to shaving, fixing his gaze again to the mirror as the razor made tracks through the white lather on his face. But I knew what he meant deep in my soul. Hearing him in that understated way spoke volumes, planting a seed so deeply in my spirit that it still grows in me now. That statement has informed my life and my "going all the way" in everything I do. Through every dream, every endeavor, every task, those powerfully simple words have stayed with me.

My first rotation in nursing school was at a geriatric home. I loved to shave the faces of the gentlemen who could not do it for themselves. As I pulled the sterile hospital razor across the face of a patient, I would reflect on those shaves with my dad and the moment he gave me the words that were shaping my life. I wondered what they had said to their daughters, and how full circle it was that I was shaving them.

After I graduated with a Bachelor of Science degree in nursing, I moved home for a couple of years. While working in the SICU (surgical intensive care unit) on twelve-hour shifts (7 p.m. to 7 a.m.) at Schumpert Memorial Hospital, I would come home sometimes so exhausted that I would fall asleep at a red light along the way. Once home, I'd soak in the tub in Mommy and Daddy's bathroom, my five-foot-ten body too long for it, but would submerge my torso for relaxation first, then alternate with my legs. As I looked to my left at the double green sinks and the white formica countertop where my dad would still shave each morning to start his day, I recalled our time and talks there. I wanted to run off stage and give my father the college diploma, the crowns, the accolades I had earned and lay them at his feet because of how his words that day became my constant source of inspiration.

CHAPTER 24

When Your Hand In The Lion's Mouth, Pat His Head

After competing for six years in pageants, I finally won the coveted title of Miss Louisiana in 1984, again the first woman of color to do so. Along the way, I was able to put my love of singing to good use, winning the crown after performing a special arrangement of "Over the Rainbow."

The Miss Louisiana pageant was part of the Miss America system of scholarship pageants, and the next competition was for that title. Talent competition was a huge component of the competition, and because Vanessa Williams broke the glass ceiling for black girls by winning the pageant in 1984, it seemed to open the door to more of us at the state level. My family believed in me and rooted for me in the nearly fifteen pageants in which I competed. Once the excitement wore off, though, I had so much preparation in the two-and-a half months to the pageant with wardrobe, trunk show, interview drills, and packing for a weeklong stay in Atlantic City with the Boardwalk parade and all the festivities surrounding it. A lovely volunteer Dorothy Hoogland accompanied me and she couldn't have been sweeter.

Six women of color competed in 1984, the most at that time in the pageant's lily white history. It was a grand thing to be there. However, the Miss America pageant still sat under the cloud of scandal that year, due to the unauthorized pictures published by Penthouse Magazine of Vanessa. For that reason, the unspoken opinion was it put the chances of another black girl winning in jeopardy. Vanessa had crowned me when I became Miss Louisiana, an amazing treat and I learned first-hand how gracious, magnanimous, and beautiful she was, and I couldn't stop staring at those amazing eyes. She and I toured the 1984 World's Fair in New Orleans together, and I had my first taste of paparazzi. By the time September arrived, my chaperone and I were headed to New Jersey and I was still determined to use the exposure the pageant afforded to assist my desired singing career, no matter what. My dad, siblings and a couple aunts, cousins, and uncles made the pilgrimage to Atlantic city to support and enthusiastically cheer me on during the week of competition. Many other fans, friends, and supporters from across the state also attended. They were hopeful and so proud of their Shreveport, Louisiana girl.

One of my pageant sisters was Maryline Blackburn, whom I call Maryl, and she was the first woman of color to win the title of Miss Alaska, where she was raised with her military family. She also beat a little-known contestant named Sarah Palin, who we'd hear about in the political arena in 2008. Because of our deep connection made during and after our Miss America journey, we stayed in touch and decided to seek out New York City together to see if we could start our post-pageant singing careers there. We were in our early twenties and trying hard to look more grown up. We planned and budgeted for a three-week stay in the Big Apple. It was my second trip to New York, and her first.

Armed with only our talents, crowns, and scepters, we met with many interested agents and managers who we hoped would work with us. We sang at open mics, saw a couple Broadway shows getting our discounted TKTS prices, and ate modest dinners. It was a fantastically memorable trip for both of us; the city felt enchanting.

One night, after singing at Catch A Rising Star's open mic, we were approached by a slender, cocoa skinned, thin gentleman with black sideburns wearing a suit. Arthur said that he loved my singing and wanted to put me on the "black vinyl." He wanted to record me! He was a promoter and extremely impressed with me. That was all fine and good, but he kept showing up at the same places we did, which creeped me out a bit. Before Maryl and I left the city, he'd found our hotel, called, and said he'd like to take us to meet Mr. Curtis Mayfield in Atlanta, Georgia, and that he would set up a recording with Curtis — one of the most influential soul singers who ever lived, and a two-time Rock & Roll Hall of Fame inductee. We were excited at this possibility, but still creeped out. We asked Arthur how he found our hotel and he said he just figured it out, which raised my creeper factor six notches. It all sounded too good to be true, but Maryl and I were cautiously optimistic.

I told Arthur he would have to clear it with my father because I wanted him to know someone was watching out for us. We were excited but a little weirded out by his omnipresence and ability to suddenly materialize while we were in New York. Because of that, Maryl and I went everywhere together. New York was a real possibility for our careers. The people we met were most interested in working with us when we moved there. I had checked into getting a nursing job to supplement my income if we moved to New York, and a place to park my new 190E Mercedes that I had recently purchased. When we left the Big Apple, Maryl went back to Alaska, and we continued to discuss where we should go and what we should do to further our careers.

I flew back home to my hospital shifts in the surgical intensive care unit. Upon my return to Shreveport, I told my dad all about our trip—who we had met, where we sang, and what a great time we'd had. I also told him about this new man we'd met who said he said he wanted to record me. Dad called him a few weeks after I returned to get a feel for him, since I had mentioned how he kept showing up wherever we were the last week of our trip. We didn't want to appear too eager, and I thought talking man-to-man would send a message of protection for his girl. I listened in the kitchen as Dad talked to Arthur on the wall-attached princess phone, hearing only his side of the conversation. Afterward, Dad said he thought Arthur could perhaps put us in touch with people who could help our careers along, but that we should stay on our "p's and q's" if we decided to go on the trip.

My dad called Arthur back a few days later to say that we were interested in meeting him in Atlanta. Arthur arranged the flight tickets, along with hotel reservations, and sent the information by mail. Maryl and I were excited to have another adventure together, this time in Atlanta. We requested a shared room, agreeing to stick together like glue during our visit.

We were scheduled to be in Atlanta for four days, a long week-end, and expected to meet Mr. Mayfield shortly after arriving, since we thought that was the purpose of the trip. Our shared room on a Marriott property was a wall away from Arthur's. He took us to some dinners in the evening, and he arranged for and did a bit of sightseeing with us, but whenever I'd politely ask when we were going to meet and record with the legend, as he had promised, Arthur would just say, "Soon."

On the third evening, while having a conversation with an old flame on our room phone, Arthur started banging on the wall. "Get off that phone!" he shouted through the paper-thin wall.

My eyes got so large as I slowly looked at Maryl, shocked by the absurdity of him yelling at me. She and I mouthed, "He's crazy!" Then Maryl said, "I think he likes you!"

"Ughhh," I said. "I sure don't like him, not like that."

Immediately, I got off the phone. Maryl and I both wondered if he had cameras in the room. Was he spying on us, too? We quietly started to look around. Since I wasn't shouting on the phone, how did Arthur know I was having a conversation? That's when I realized he was listening to us through the wall. I was taken aback and frankly a little afraid, but happy to have that wall between us. Feeling controlled, I immediately wanted to go home, but he held our return tickets in his possession. Because of that, and his demands we not go anywhere without letting him know, even downstairs to the lobby or gift shop, I did not like this situation. I shifted from scared to madder than a wet hen. Part of me wanted to yell through the wall, "You don't own me! You don't get to tell me when I can have a conversation and where I can go just because you brought us here!"

Instead, I called my dad from the phone in the room, so livid that I paced in between the double beds as far as the phone line would allow, as we talked. Maryl lay on the bed, pulled out a magazine, and listened to my side of the conversation.

"Daddy," I whispered, "This weirdo is telling us when we can and cannot talk on the phone. We haven't even met Mr. Mayfield yet and we've been here two days; he is very controlling and I want to just leave and forget all this!"

Dad, in his saucy southern style with a lilting drawl, a bit of teacher and hint of preacher, said, "Now, baby, when you got your hand in the lion's mouth, you gotta pat his head. He has something you need, so until you get it, don't act a monkey, just play along. Your ticket has you coming home in a day or so. Stay together with Maryline and be cool." He repeated that last part: "Just be cool. You'll be home soon." Always the voice of reason.

I took a deep breath. "Okay Daddy, I'll try."

"You call me anytime and be smart. I will come and get you if I need to," Dad added.

"Thank you, Daddy," I said calmed and reassured, loving how he seemed to understand how not to inflame the situation more. Just hearing his voice and wise words was a cooling salve to my anger.

I relayed the words Dad had given to Maryl. As we sat in a short silence, looking at each other, we both knew this situation was strange and uncomfortable. But Dad's words got me off the ledge. I still felt incensed at Arthur's chastising and monitoring of our conversations.

Maryl and I sat across the bed from each other and whispered quietly, making a pact about how we would handle ourselves until we could get to the airport and out of Atlanta. We knew we needed to stay calm, as Dad had said, and put on our poker faces at least until we got the chance to meet Mr. Curtis Mayfield, though we weren't sure that was really happening. We did jumping jacks in the room to work out the anger and disintegrated into hysterical laughter at the craziness of the situation we found ourselves in. But we didn't like it.

Arthur hit on the wall again. "What are you girls laughing about?" he yelled through the thin wall between our rooms. We stopped, looked at each other, and laughed some more, and then laughed harder, because it was absurd. But what else could we do?

On the fourth day, we met in the lobby and played along with the plan we'd set. We said hello with nonchalant nice smiles and acted very excited about the unknown day he planned for us. We even asked how he slept. Though he had been honorable, getting the plane tickets, the hotel, all done openly, the sneaking concern that he would try to do something like make an inappropriate move, or kidnap us, crossed my mind. I was on high alert, wanting to be sure he was not a wolf in sheep's clothing. Without showing our anger or impatience, we got into the car and pinched each other in the back seat, a reminder to keep playing it cool, because we were on our last day there. Inside, though, I wanted to punch him. Plus, I was armed with my dad's words — and a pair of scissors I requested from the front desk, now stowed in my purse in case Arthur acted crazy and I needed to defend us. We left our suitcases packed in the room with a "Do Not Disturb" sign on the door.

A hired car service drove us around Atlanta. Arthur would sit in the front passenger seat with us in the back. After some late morning sightseeing, and to our surprise, he announced we were going to the home and studio of Mr. Curtis Mayfield. But the bigger surprise? We were a surprise to him. Mr. Mayfield had not been told we were going to sing or that he was going to record us! Arthur pumped me up to think we were coming to sign a record deal. Lord, we were so green.

We didn't really know what to expect. When we got there, Mr. Mayfield opened a side door. When I saw him, his hit song "Superfly" suddenly played in my head. I smiled. He invited us into a small studio. Maryl and I sat together on the piano stool while Mr. Mayfield sat across from us on one end of the sofa, with Arthur sat on the other. We introduced ourselves and he started some benign chitchat. Being pageant girls, we were accustomed to talking to any and everyone, so that part was easy. But we didn't talk about music.

He asked us if we wanted something to eat, which I thought was nice. I also thought, Did we come here to eat? Or am I about to get asked to sing or be signed? Again, I had no idea how it all worked, but I wanted to learn the process and not jump to any conclusions. Then, finally, he asked, "So you guys sing or something?"

Maryl and I looked at each other like, You don't know? Didn't that Arthur man tell you why we're here? "Yes, we sing, not together usually, but we do sing," we mumbled over each other, trying to be polite. What I didn't say was, That's why we're here!

Then he asked us to sing something. We sang a simple church song duet, unrehearsed, because we had no accompaniment tracks and I only knew how to play church songs. We followed that with a little solo for each of us, so nondescript I don't recall the song. In New York, there were always bands that knew familiar songs at the open mic places. Here, we had only the air to play for us. How I wished I had let it rip, just sang out assured and confident like I knew how to do, but I did not. We didn't know how to prepare, because we naively thought it was all set up by "Mr. Weirdo". Though we were still confused by this casual visit, we wanted to make an impression, which I don't think we did.

All he said was, "Nice, girls, nice," which said to me, No, girls, no.

Mr. Mayfield left the room for a bit, then came back and said how nice it was to meet us. He wished us good luck. I had to fix my face, because I wasn't sure if this was a rejection or a "just not right now" situation. We were gracious, smiled our pageant smiles, and thanked him for his time and attention, which of course we meant. And for lunch.

No recording. No talk of a record deal. I wanted to ask, "What now?" to Arthur, but didn't know if we should ask, since we were even more confused. We'd had a visit, like regular houseguests whose friend brings them to meet a famous musician, punctuated by a song interlude to finish lunch. We had hoped for something more—some hope, some "Come back again," or "You have potential," or "I want to work with you in the studio", since we were both beginning our singing careers post-crowns. Arthur had built up the visit to be so much more. We were floored, figuring the talk of putting me on the "black vinyl" was perhaps just a ploy to impress me. It was clear that Arthur liked me, and I was equally clear that I was not interested in him. At all.

The ride back to the hotel was quiet. Then I said, "That was an interesting meeting. Thank you for making the introduction."

He took us back to the hotel. We walked up to our room, grabbed our suitcases and changed clothes, and walked back to the car. We got into the awaiting car; Arthur still held our return tickets. Not until we got on the road to the airport did he hand them to us. We were eager for this trip to be over and have distance from Arthur and his antics. I didn't feel as grateful as I should, because we felt he'd baited us. I regret not taking in the meeting with Mr. Curtis Mayfield for what it was, but I couldn't get out of the car fast enough. As soon as the driver pulled up to the curbside, we hopped out of that car with a little too much enthusiasm.

I had what I wanted, my ticket home. Though some choice words for Arthur poured through me, I held my tongue and didn't "act a monkey." I had patted the lion's head and gotten my hand out of his mouth, like Daddy said. The best part, retrospectively, was that we actually sat for an hour or more in the presence of the legendary Mr. Curtis Mayfield.

CHAPTER 25
Ain't No Man Worth All That

Our parents, particularly Dad, were very protective of their growing, sprouting, blooming daughters. He wanted us to model our mother, who was so kind, virtuous, sweet-natured, and quite a snappy dresser. When we were leaving the house in the mornings, if our skirts were shorter than above the knee or, heaven forbid, slightly see-through, Dad would calmly ask us to put on a slip, or he'd ask, "Where's the rest of your dress?"

I was always obedient, but learned later that my sisters Kathy and Alene would change back into whatever outfits they'd had to remove at home once they got to school. It never occurred to me that I could do that. Dad always wanted us to carry ourselves with a certain grace and dignity, though at some point we all rebelled a little. Our dad held us to a high standard; his girls were to carry themselves like ladies.

Alene was the first girl born in our big extended Whitaker/White family. Because my mother was the eldest daughter of her family, she got special visits from the grandparents, uncles, and aunts. I have heard the stories of how our maternal grandfather Poppa Buddy would stop by our home on 73rd Street after work just to hold her and get a kiss. She was what was called in the black community a "high yella baby," referring to her lighter brown skin. A beautiful baby, born three year after Jr., she grew into a headstrong, pretty, willful, and athletic girl.

Alene was a majorette in high school, played softball, and played oboe in the marching band. When we hosted ladies from our church for the mission meeting at our house, a bible study for women with community outreach, I would overhear some of the ladies mentioning under their breath how Alene was "mannish" or "fast" in her teens. Mannish meant their impression was that she liked the attention of men. She was a pretty girl who loved to dress in the fashions of the day, which included daisy duke shorts, a halter top in summer, beehive hairdos, light makeup (mostly eyeliner and powder), and a little lip gloss. Though she gave Dad some pushback because she didn't always conform to his way of dressing or demure behavior, I thought she was absolutely gorgeous and self-assured. I longed to be that confident when I watched her move about. She played the piano, looked like a magazine cover girl, ran like a boy—and could fight like one, too. Because she also enjoyed her femininity, she got cat-called a lot, and some boys thought they could touch her if they chose.

That never turned out well for them. She punched one guy during junior high, breaking his glasses and leaving him with a black eye, and another in high school who tried to touch her inappropriately. However she was provoked, or how bewildered my parents were at times with her nonconformity, they had to pay for those glasses but she was not one to stand down. I loved her feistiness. Though she wasn't the typical sweet make-nice Louisiana girl, I believe they quietly loved that she stood up for herself. She also had to fight in high school because her school was newly integrated, and she was one of the unwelcomed new black kids integrating Captain Shreve High School in the early '70s.

In her early adult life, my sister found herself in a situation with someone she was dating. He told her he had broken it off with his ex, but in reality, had not. She was caught in a web, trying to get the guy to be with her and losing sight of herself. She was becoming someone she didn't recognize in her attempts to win his exclusive affection. Dad patiently watched this escalating situation for a time, then stepped in to remind her that she was never second best and to carry herself like the princess she was. He said to her, within earshot of me, "If a young man doesn't know the jewel that you are, it's time to move on. Act like a lady, keep your head held up, and get to stepping!"

One night in my early twenties, after moving back home to save money after nursing school, I was crying hard after a breakup, sipping on a weak glass of cheap wine and listening to Whitney Houston sing, "All at Once" in my childhood bedroom. I learned that after a two-year relationship, my then-boyfriend had been a cheater-cheater pumpkin eater, with a girl that I knew. It was a hard, snot-hanging, ugly cry, the cry of a young broken betrayed heart. Whitney's warm rich vocals caressed, addressed, and encouraged even harder tears over the stark reality of my situation.

My door was closed. The music and the muffled sobs weren't too loud, because I didn't want my dad to know that another boyfriend had shown his true colors. He'd held serious reservations about this one from the "git go," but had trusted and encouraged me always to be observant and smart, because "a man is measured way more by what he does than what he says."

He must have heard my crying after all, because he gently opened the door. "What's this all about, Nita?" he asked.

From my dark room, lit by only a single glowing candle, I looked up at him with swollen, wet, puffy eyes. I tried to explain between sobs underscored by the Whitney's soaring vocals and music that I was heartbroken. "I feel so deceived... and so deeply hurt," I sniffled, the pitch of my voice rising with every word. I took a break to wipe my nose. "How could he do this? With one of my sorority sisters?!"

I finally let out a big wail that had been brewing. My breathing shortened into wet gasps. I braced myself for him to say, "I told you so."

Without raising an eyebrow, he simply said, "Now that's enough of that. You go on and get your cry out, but you listen. If he treated you like that, disrespected you, and lied, he didn't deserve you anyway, Ain't no man worth all that." he admonished.

He walked back down the hall to his room. The simplicity of his words stunned me and seemed to suck my tears back into my eyes. I pushed "stop" on the cassette player and sat in the loud silence for a moment, taking in what he'd just said. Then I pushed "play" again.

I couldn't hear Whitney anymore, just the sound of my heart beating as the last tears dried. I wiped my snotty wet upper lip and nose with the back of my hand, took another sip of the cheap Asti Spumante wine, then got up to wash my face and hands. His words fell on me like a security blanket as I lay still in my bed, starring at the ceiling, head throbbing, making short triplet inhalations like a baby that cried too hard. They wrapped me in an armor with which I would awaken, though my heart was still quite fragile. Somehow, I fell asleep.

Dad didn't say anything about my bout of crying the next day. But he reminded me of my worth by saying, "You're a lady and a queen. Don't forget." Emotionally exhausted and puffy-eyed from my hard cry, I put on my poker face and headed out for the day. I decided that I needed to wipe the slate clean of that entanglement and that's just what I did.

For a moment, I had forgotten my own value. After that, I never did again. "I am a lady, and I am the prize, just like you raised me to be," I said to myself that day.

Check. Got it, Dad.

Teenage sister Alene Whitaker

CHAPTER 26
Don't Always Be Available

There were times when my dad tried to teach me about the ways of men without making it so obvious they are mostly after the almighty "coochie" or the "vajayjay." But, more than that, I know the deeper message was about valuing myself so that I didn't give myself away too easily. He hoped he'd shown us how a gentleman should treat a woman by the way he treated Mom.

And us. From the time mother passed, he served as both mother and father, and, of course, was fiercely protective of us. The social mores of the time he dated Mom had evolved, but when I started to date after Mommy died, he, too, was a dating man. He had girlfriends while I was in college being newly widowed, and we felt protective but wanted him to be happy too. My sister Kathy and Alene didn't like one of his girlfriends and let him know it. So it was an awkward place to dispense dating standards while dating. Still, he'd slip some wisdom in during our shave chats or while we were talking on the phone. For a while, he thought I had a "broken picker", because the guys that were attracted to me were in some way fractured from their childhoods, and he thought I was trying to fix them.

I dated a boy while in college who graduated and moved to Wisconsin for an engineering job. Sometimes I'd wait for his phone call instead of doing something I had planned. "Too eager," Dad would say. "You got to live your life while he is living his."

After I moved to Los Angeles and met Don (who would become my husband), Dad harbored some reservations because he had not met Don and couldn't get a true sense of who he was. After I broke it to Dad gently that I was dating…wait for it…a white guy, and he was older and shorter, but the kindest, most gentle generous person, I expected some kind of reaction. He had always said that "people are just people," and I knew that gave me the freedom to choose who my heart would fall in love with. Period.

After meeting Don, and despite his concern that Don liked to drink a little, Dad proclaimed that he could see his big heart. Even so, being older and wiser, Dad slipped me some worldly wisdom in bite-sized doses so it would go down easy and stick. His concern was that Don would honor me and that I not be expected to do all the work in the relationship. He felt the fella needed to earn my attention and my affection. He was right.

Though I lived eighteen hundred miles away after I moved to California, Dad still had my ear. I listened deeply to what he had to say. "Nita, when you're dating a man, don't be too available."

I did not understand fully what he meant. Of course, when you are falling for someone, the thing you want to do most is to be together to learn more about each other; you want to talk late into the night. He cautioned me not to get swept up in all the wining and dining and repeated, "Just don't always be available."

He continued, "When a man calls and asks you out or to meet him, sometimes say you have somethin' to do or some other plans, even if you have nothin' to do. You could be sitting at home, but you don't want to run every time they call because you need to let them work to earn you." I was quiet and thought about what he said. "Keep a little of your life for yourself; it keeps him wanting you all the more."

Don would call some afternoons and ask if I wanted to meet him for dinner and a movie. Usually he took me to a very expensive restaurant, probably out of my registered nurse budget, but I heeded and needed Dad's advice, even though it meant I spent several evenings alone twiddling my thumbs, watching television, or eating Bob's Big Boy's hamburgers or Taco Bell. Dad raised us to be independent and was careful to teach us that a man is not the first ingredient for a happy life. That has to come from within.

When my daughters reached dating age, I tried to teach them the lesson about not being too available. That wasn't easy, because their dad wasn't around to give his advice or perspective. He had raised the bar high for them, and hoped they would expect to be adored and treated by their fellas in the loving adoring ways he had treated me. I'd tell them how easy it is to get lost inside another person when you're dating, and how that person can become the center of your world. The words of my father fell out of my mouth: "Just don't always be available. Don't give all of you away until you know that this person is worthy of your heart. Sometimes people can take that willingness for weakness."

Five years after Don passed, fate walked me into a supper club, where a lovely sweet man was serendipitously seated at my table. I had told my friends and family that I would never love or marry again, but God had other plans. Well, a sweet, smart, silly, Southern Sagittarian man named Scott Perkins made me the object of his affection as a new love danced and swooned our hearts, holding us in her embrace.

Scott came as unexpected as an afternoon shower, and felt as right as rain. It happened like the blush of a new teen romance complete with butterflies, late-night giggles, a renewed aliveness, and great anticipation. He was white, chivalrous, tall and handsome, and not in the business. He had a simple kindness and was an engineer who wore crazy socks, had Paul McCartney hair, was a divorced dad of a grown son and was working in New York on a Hurricane Sandy disaster recovery project. My family and friends were hesitantly happy for me because he seemed to come out of nowhere and they had only known me with Don. This was an adjustment for my village. And who was this Louisiana white boy taking up space in my life and heart? Even though I had been alone and not dated for five years, my people were still cautiously optimistic and protective for me and my girls. My dad first asked me if I was ready, but later said that he knew I was smart, and trusted my decisions. I too was reluctant at first, but as we went, and I could let go a little, love slowly washed over me like a warm shower and I allowed it to fill some of the places of my broken heart . . . and his. After a friend's husband died suddenly, I decided to give love a try. We fell fast. To feel love again and to feel alive has felt liberating. We've been together almost seven years now, and he has been a lovely blessing and addition to my life.

Still, I remembered the words of my dad in the early days of our whirlwind romance. Truthfully, a lot of it flew out the window, because we were a long-distance couple and didn't have the luxury of being unavailable. But my Dad's words taught me so much about how to conduct myself with the opposite sex—and how not to. And to keep a little of myself for myself. That level of unavailability helps a girl remember that she is a prize to be won.

CHAPTER 27

Keep A Check With Your Name On It

Dad has always had the gift of giving me a profound life lesson with a few simple words. One time, we were watching some part of a television program where a dejected wife whose husband had either died or left, was grieving and was overwhelmingly sad. She had not understood all the financial implications she faced now that he was gone, and didn't know where their money was, how much she had left, or if he had spent it all.

Dad was surprised because he had seen his mother and father working alongside each other, and he and my mother had done the same. They were life partners, with one hand knowing what the other was doing, as both handled the full finances and concerns of the family. He was among the non-traditional thinkers of his generation who were lovingly accepting of women having children and working outside of the home simultaneously; Mother worked full time while they raised the four of us. He taught us to drive a stick shift (the first one was in the collar of an old Chevy truck), to check the oil in our cars, to pump our own gas, how to paint a house and a room, how to save our earnings, how to steer if we hit rain or black ice in winter, and how to change a tire and fix a leaky faucet; things to help us survive and thrive on our own.

After we watched that program, he took it all in and gave me a piece of advice I never forgot: "I don't mind if you marry a Rockefeller or a poor man, as long as they are good kind people. But you keep a check with your name on it." He wanted us to know that even if we married someone of great means, it was important that we earn our own money, even if it wasn't a necessity for us to work, and that it was important to be involved with the finances in a relationship.

That stayed with me. I have said the same things to my daughters.

I understand first-hand how being your own breadwinner, or at least a contributor, gives you a sense of your own value. As a woman who has always worked and raised children, it is a great feeling to be able to take care of yourself financially and contribute to the household. That is not to say there is not equal value in a partner or spouse who chooses to stay home and be a housewife or househusband, but if a woman is wired for working and derives great satisfaction from it, I believe that what my daddy said is true: a check with her name on it allows her to feel a different kind of contribution to her own life, her independence and her self-reliance.

CHAPTER 28
Make Room In Your Life For You
———

Every Saturday when we were growing up, my dad would mow the quarter-acre front and back lawns of our home, sometimes twice a week in summer. He also edged the lawns with small shoveled expertise, de-weeded the flower beds, and trimmed the hedges. Dad always gave mother a sweet kiss before he went out for any yard work, and again when he returned inside. Sometimes, he'd sing while he mowed and edged. On especially hot days, Mother would have us bring him a glass of cold water. He took great pride keeping the yard manicured, planting annuals and trimming the front shrubbery, but what I didn't grasp then, was that this time was *his* time.

Dad worked many jobs and I never knew him to be unemployed. He kept a rhythm to his day. It started with his morning school bus route picking up and delivering children to their schools. When he came home from the morning route, he'd do chores around the house, do some debit insurance collection (he became the top selling agent in the region for thirty years), and some days sell Stuart McGuire shoes door to door. Then he'd get on his bus for the late afternoon drop-offs from school. More than once, he brought home a stray kitten or puppy he'd found. I would be so excited.

It wasn't until I had a few sick days from school that I saw his routine that included a little time, whenever possible, to watch part of his favorite soap, General Hospital. He'd set an alarm and take a short power nap before getting up to drive the bus for the 2:30 school pickup. There, he'd load up children and reverse his morning routine finishing with an empty bus. After his bus route ended, he'd head to his final janitorial job at the electric company offices or at Sears for a few years, until 9 p.m. Often, I wondered how my dad stayed powered up for the long days that continued after his bus route was done.

My high school senior classes were done for me around 11:30. I would come home until the last hour of school for cheerleading practice, so I got to see a little more of his day.

Dad knelt each night to say his prayers and spend some time alone with God; he has done this since he was a little boy. After his first knee replacement surgery at seventy, and its many ensuing complications, he did not get back his full range of motion so he began to sit on the side of his bed with his bible for this prayer and meditation time, his door slightly ajar.

We all came to understand what this sacred time was for him, and still is a time he sets aside to re-center and connect to his source and faith.

Whenever my dad visited my family in California, many of our friends wanted to make sure they got to see him. My dear friend whom I call my brother Charles Randolph-Wright, the godfather to our youngest daughter Liisi, reminded me of a chat he'd had with Dad during one of his visits and a holiday gathering. Dad, always eager to engage with the friends and family in our Los Angeles village, asked Charles how things were going and what he was up to. Charles, who later would direct Motown, the Musical on Broadway, told him about all the projects he was working on, things he needed to get done, the meetings he had scheduled; all the things an emerging writer and director had on his plate.

After listening, Dad gently interrupted. "Now Charles, make sho' you make room in your life for you, cause that's what'll keep you in balance." He then added, "A bobtail dog can't walk on a log without that tail to keep his balance. He gon' fall off that thang!"

His words stopped Charles in his tracks. Dad broke it down further, adding, "You see son, people will use you up if you let 'em. They will pull on you, ask for extra things, and more of your time. And sometimes you can't let folk know how smart you really are, because they will tap out your resources. So, whether it's work or with family and friends, you gotta keep some of your time and your smarts just for you to take care of yourself, and not rush to please all those people all the time."

All Charles could say was, "Whooh! That's so good, Mr. Green, I will remember that."

Those words he didn't know he needed to hear had come from a man who deeply understood the value of a person's own time. Dad gave him a smile, looking him kindly in the eyes, and laid his large gentle hand on Charles' shoulder. "You do that, son." Then he was pulled away by someone else who wanted a word with him.

In that moment, it became crystal clear for me that my dad had cleverly developed his own "me time", the time he kept for himself long ago despite the many titles, hats, jobs, and roles he juggled. Perhaps those moments of mowing or praying, or his mindless time watching his soap opera or taking a nap, were how he kept some balance and recharged during all those years when no one even knew the word mindfulness or talked of a balanced life. And Charles took that piece of practical wisdom and incorporated some "me-time" into this life with Dad's words laying that foundation.

He phoned me one evening when I was parenting my then school-aged daughters, picking up and dropping off, running here and there with the girls' school activities, cooking meals, running a household, managing employees, and minding my own singing and acting career. "Girl, you gon' wear yourself plumb out! You made me tired just hearing all this," he chuckled. "Remember to take some time for yo'self, make room in your life for You." I knew then and now that I am still learning to do that.

"Thank you for the reminder Daddy," I said.

"Night baby, now get some rest. Love you."

"Love you. Daddy."

CHAPTER 29

Keep Gettin' Up

When my mother died, a gaping hole was left in our world. She was the light, the glue, the big thinker, the children's advocate and Vacation Bible School coordinator, the consumer guide reader, and the perfect team partner for my father. Instinctually and spiritually, he knew he would have to lead our family through her passing, even as he grieved.

Our family sat in a surreal disbelief in those first weeks — and then life moved us on. My brother, who had always lived with my father, decided he would stay in the home with Dad. They both were working, but the emotional support of being there for each other was heartwarming. Junior told me of a spiritual visitation from mother that all of us longed for; that she came and sat on the edge of his bed and reassured him that he would be okay and that she was, too. This was of great comfort to him and made him feel so special. Dad and Junior still live together in a loving, supportive way.

When Mom died, I was numb and angry, not accepting that someone so loving, giving and amazing could die at age forty-nine. How could she not meet my someday husband and my yet-to-be-had babies? It wasn't fair, and I felt mad at God for taking her from me, from my family. None of us know how to express that except through tears, anger, silence...all the steps to acceptance.

Dad insisted that I get back to college, having already missed two weeks during my first semester, because he knew how important my college was to my mother. The love that we shared for our mother was the emotional bond that got us through that first year and those beyond. Our family became closer. Because the grief was so individual, we had to hold on to what was left, which was one another. Dad was steadfast in his devotion, not letting anything or anyone get in the middle of our family. He became the glue, and filled in as best he could to be both mother and father for all of us.

I watched him begin again with a heavy heart and valiantly continued a life without his thirty-one-year partner, still parenting his nearly adult children.

Don LaFontaine and I often thought it funny how our two voices found each other in the City of Angels, a city of four million. Widowed in 2008 — I turned right to my father to guide me through and help me move forward from his own parallel lived experience. A master at his craft of voice-over, the Voice of Movie Trailers, and his immortal "In a world...," the opening line to countless trailers and commercials ensures his legacy today and likely forever in the world of entertainment. I couldn't fathom living in a world, without him. The world around me felt surreal. It was difficult to grasp how life was moving all about me, yet my own felt completely stopped. But at my dad's urging to get the girls back to some kind of normalcy, I sent them back to their schools. I did so with a heavy heart. I wanted to keep them cocooned, because I knew no other kids at their respective schools had experienced the loss of a parent and couldn't know how to console them. The unimaginable had happened to us, and only we or someone else who had been through it could truly understand. I spoke with their teachers and asked them to keep an eye out for varied behavior in the girls. Children truly grieve differently, and I didn't know when to expect an avalanche of tears, uneasy quiet, or wild rebellion as the loss sank in.

Three weeks after the loss, following the burial, the celebration of life service, and all the markers we did to acknowledge his amazing life, we tried to begin again. I'd drop the girls at school and we were greeted with love from all who knew what we'd been through. They showed great empathy though none of her classmates had lost a parent. Then I'd drive to the nearest Target or grocery store or whatever was open just to wander around, buying things we needed. Or didn't. I'd get some retail therapy, but mostly, I was just killing time. Our wonderful housekeeper whom I referred to as my "other wife", Maria Herrera, was holding down the fort even in her grief, and our beloved Aunt Lillian Whitaker (one of my mother's closest sisters who had married Uncle Roy, and was like a grandmother to the girls) insisted on staying a few weeks more as the many people that had filled our home for nearly two weeks had to get back to their own lives. The crowds were gone and it was time for me to take the helm of our new lives in uncharted waters, with a sorely missing oar. My dad had done the same. There was so much to do, so much to handle. I had to find a new rhythm and continue to raise my teenage daughters while I, too, was grieving. I am not the only person ever to have traveled this road, but when you are on it, it seems endless and overwhelming and alone. Life goes in slow motion.

I called my dad often and asked him how he made it through after Momma died, where he got the strength to keep going. I wanted to glean some of his strength for myself; needed to hear from someone close who had survived the loss of a spouse and then had to carry on raising kids. Some days, I'd drive around in the parking lot of unopened stores because I was too sad to go home to a house, where my Don would never again be. I'd just drive in circles and talk to my dad as I cried. I'd say, "I don't know how to do this, Daddy. I don't know if I can; if I am strong enough."

I just wanted to go to bed and stay there for a long while. As they say down home, I wanted to "take to the bed." The lion of grief roared and frightened me. More than tremendous sadness, I felt afraid. How would I keep them safe?

But I instinctively knew that if I fell apart, if I went down, who would hold up my children? How could I be there to comfort them and carry them forward?

My dad, with his gentle wisdom, calmly talked to me as I drove in lazy circles one particularly difficult day.

"The Bible teaches that in life, we will be going into a storm, be in the middle of one, or coming out of one. That's just life. Now you've been in a storm and you are trying to get to the other side of it. I know it's hard, baby girl, but you gon' make it. I did, and you will, too. Daddy's praying for you and the girls every night and day. Just keep gettin' up, baby girl. That bed is gonna try to hold you and you gon' grieve, but you gotta keep gettin' up and get into life; be 'round people. You gon' make it."

Those words— "keep gettin' up"—became a strong, quiet mantra within me during that first year that otherwise felt like a blur. They kept me rising and pushing to get into the sunshine. And wasn't it my job to show my girls how to play again after a storm? We had been through what felt like a tsunami and the deafening silence that followed, and I had to lead them to the light of life again. I needed to be the example.

My family and village were beyond amazing in how they rallied around us. The calls kept coming, friends brought food and put me out front to sing when I didn't want to or knew if I could, and my girls' school friends rallied around them like I had never seen. The outpouring of kindness and genuine concern was beautiful to watch even then, as well as retrospectively, seeing how they all loved us and pulled us up out of the mountain of grief toward some new normal life to which we were adjusting.

Life can deal a heavy hand. Some storms take you under. But as I am reminded even now, nearly thirteen years later, to keep getting up. You're gonna make it. It is the rising up that causes you to win. Find something to do. Help somebody else and keep gettin' up in the fight for your life, your light, and your spirit.

CHAPTER 30
You Come From A Can-Do People

Dad has always been my biggest fan and supporter. His center always seemed to be filled with joy, forever resilient, an indomitable spirit with an infectious get-up-and-go attitude. He would remind us that we could do anything we put our minds to. If our brother Junior could go out and get a regular job despite his special needs, we could shoot for the moon. He prayed nightly for the health, safety, and success of our children and us, and for our dreams to be realized. As a grown woman with children, I've called him many times to ask for his counsel, because his advice is always direct and simple, wise and calming.

My baby girl, Liisi, came here seemingly as an old spirit. Quiet and thumb-sucking, she was observant and went from being shyly mute in public to telling us everything everyone said from the comfort of the car ride. She grew from being a quiet little one to a very funny girl with a big personality, four years and two days younger than her sister. Skye, our first born was also a thumb sucker whose sparkly personality and early command of language helped her become an early reader. Bursting into her kindergarten class with flair, her classmates gathered saying, "Skye's here!" She came here precocious, energetic, engaging, and always in motion, even though she would later grow quieter with a shy side emerging; both girls unique and equally delightful.

We moved Skye from her beloved Waldorf school, where she had been kind of a rock star because she entered kindergarten reading when most of her peers did not. She'd also enjoyed the freedom to run and play and grow with her other twenty-nine classmates and friends. It was not an easy decision to make, because she'd spent seven years at Waldorf growing in mind, body, friendships and spirit, but there were academic holes in her education, and because of issues with her teacher by the time we left, her self-esteem had taken a hit. Her Dad and I felt she needed a different school experience. She entered sixth grade at her new school feeling shy, quiet, and uncertain.

As she adjusted and made a few new friends in her new Pasadena Episcopal School, we learned there was an opportunity to participate in a citywide essay contest. It was a hard transition for her. She was sorely missing her friends, and we thought this would be a way for her to connect and stand out, since she excelled at anything involving reading and performance. Skye felt it was such a long shot because of so many entries that she would not have a realistic chance to win. That someone else would be given the shot and not her, played like a broken record in the house. Though she didn't enjoy competitions, per se, this was different because it required her to write about how Dr. Martin Luther King's message of non-violence, equality, and education could make the world a better place.

After some nudging, she wrote and rewrote what she wanted to say. When she read it to us at home, I cried. Because our family was interracial, we'd often spoken to her about how we were the "dream" that Dr. King talked about, how it was a crime at one time for her Dad and me to be together, and how like the Loving family who helped change the law in 1967, our hearts didn't see color, just love. We lived by the mantra of judging people by the content of their character. Maybe she got it, we hoped.

She submitted her essay with hundreds of entries from other schools and didn't think about it much after. I was proud that she'd entered and taken a chance. A few weeks later, we learned her essay was chosen for the finals and she'd have to go and read it to a live audience and judges. She was nervously excited.

Even though she could appear shy, when she got on a stage, she became more of her true nature; a loving, fluent, effervescent, articulate girl. She loved being on the stage, even when it was shared, and if there was a physical spotlight, she absolutely loved the feeling of the blinding warm light, where she couldn't see the audience's faces. Now, she would be up there alone, without a spotlight or a group to surround her in a sterile auditorium and this frightened her the most.

On the drive to the event, she was one big bundle of nerves, which just revved up the fear quotient. I had called my dad earlier to let him know what she was about to do and how nervous she was and knowing the sound of his voice would calm her. He said, "Call me when she gets in the car." Skye's dad was meeting us there, so I called my father while I was driving and put him on speakerphone so Skye could hear him. Liisi was there listening and always absorbing as an observant child.

"Hi Poppa!" she said, hearing his voice.

"Hi, baby! Your momma says there is this contest you have to speak at today. Now, remember, you been performing in front of people all yo' life, so this is nothing new. Started singing songs for everybody when you was two. Now, you come from a can-do people, and you can do anything you set your mind to. Show 'em what you come from! I had to walk a mile to school in shoes that had holes in the bottom and still made a life. You have that drive in your veins. You can do this thing, so you go on in there and do what you do."

We could hear the smile in his voice and I could see his dimpled cheek and hear him chuckle. Skye smiled broadly and said, "Okay, Poppa, I will!"

His words soothed her nerves and boosted her confidence at the same time.

We gathered in a room full of people from different schools, parents, friends, school officials, and a group of judges seated in front. All twelve finalists were invited. The head of Skye's school Dr. Olson sat in the audience for support, which made Skye more nervous. The twelve finalists were seated on the front row to the right in a small auditorium, with a long desk set in the center of the room with a panel of six judges. There was a podium with a microphone from which each student would read. I looked over to her and mouthed the words, "You can do this. Just breathe."

Then it was her turn. As she began to read her essay, her voice shaking as though it would break, knees knocking, I thought I would cry for her so that she wouldn't. It was a mix of nerves and passion in her shaky voice as she read her essay, on the brink of tears about what the words of Dr. King meant to her. We had taught our children that our family was the dream that he spoke about all those years ago. Her understanding of some of those principles came through her written words in the sixth grade.

I was more nervous than she was, and I wanted her to succeed by having a good speech and feeling she had done a good job. I was holding my breath and praying she would make it through — and she did. Her dad and I squeezed each other's hands as she made her way to her seat, feeling proud of what she had written and how she delivered it.

Judging and deliberation followed and then it was announced Skye had won! She was really surprised, overjoyed, and needed that validation of self-worth more than a high mark of a good grade.

Because of that win, she ended up sharing her essay at several churches and events with her family in tow. Some of the prizes included a letter from the governor, a trophy, a laminated certificate, and prize money, which meant a lot to her and her confidence. Along with the prestige of being the winner, she was thrilled by what she had accomplished, along with her upgraded status and confidence at her new school. If she had not tried, she would never have experienced this victory, which reinforced the belief that she, indeed, was a "can-do people," too. This was the first of many times her Poppa's inspiring words pushed them both to remember the shoulders on which they stood, and the legacy they would create in the work and words they would leave behind.

The night before and after the essay, their father did what he had done since they were little girls: he blew them a dream. After tooth brushing and snuggles and a shared chapter of a book, he had started a ritual where they would open their mouths, and he would blow a pursed mouth stream of air into theirs and they'd swallow it and smile.

Then off to sleep they'd go to chase that sweet dream. Some nights when we'd forget, they would remind him, "Daddy, you didn't blow me a dream." I'd like to think that my dad figuratively blew me lots of dreams and a can-do spirit that we passed on and blew to my girls from him.

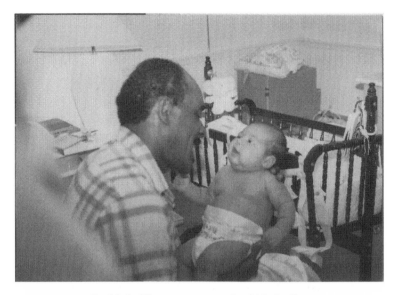

Daddy holding my two-month-old baby Skye

Daddy with my two-month-old baby Liisi

CHAPTER 31
Be As Good A Loser As You Are A Winner

One of the hard things I had to learn as a parent is how to sit with my children in the discomfort of a loss or a disappointment, such as when their team gets defeated, when they don't win the grand prize, or when they aren't elected to the position they petitioned for. It is not the most comfortable place to sit. When my daughter Skye was six and seven, she played on an American youth soccer team (AYSO). We felt that team sports would teach some gentle life skills, like teamwork and confidence. She was always running, with energy to burn, so we thought this would be a good outlet for her physical expression. We wanted to give it a try.

Another thing we felt important was how the team learned to shake the hands of the opposing players after every game, no matter who won. I thought this was a good example of sportsmanly conduct and good character building that would spill over into all parts of her life. Like my parents had done, we tried to give our children many doors to explore their interests and expand any natural abilities they showed.

At her Waldorf school in her elementary years, Skye so enjoyed games classes that were woven into the curriculum. In fifth grade, she participated in a statewide Waldorf event called the Pentathlon Games, loosely based on five original athletic events from ancient Greek mythology competitions: a discus, javelin, the long jump, wrestling, and stadion (a short foot race). That ten-year-old excelled, winning three of the events and placed highly in the others. She seemed to have natural athletic abilities. Her reward? A prestigious small simple red rose added to her head wreath.

Again, the students were encouraged to greet other competitors, whether they finished on top or not. These were good lessons that we hoped would stick for conduct whether winning or losing.

In third grade, my daughter auditioned for her school play and wanted the lead of Odysseus. Terribly upset she didn't get the part, despite the fact she'd already memorized her lines, she cried on the way home. Though disappointed, Skye enjoyed the process of learning and performing in the play so much that it ended up being a great experience. Initially, though, she was not a gracious loser, because she believed that she could perform that role better than anyone else. And she could. Her teacher, trying to mitigate her grand ambition, thought another kid would learn more from getting the lead. In the end, Skye was happy to be in the play, because she felt so alive on stage. She yearned for a chance to shine in her happy place. When she auditioned for young Nala in Lion King's Los Angeles company. She was somewhat thrown when the pianist played a different part of the song that she had not rehearsed, and my little nine-year-old got lost. This was a girl who knew a hundred songs by the time she was two; she knew she could sing it but she knew that she'd had a not good enough audition. When she walked out I saw the disappointment on her face and she told me what happened. I reassured her that it wasn't her fault but she begged me to take her back so she could redo it. And being a dramatic Gemini, she cried big. That was a tough drive home. Somewhere in there was a lesson I suppose of humility, and overall it surely made her more resilient.

Both my girls competed and participated in summer theater camps, local theater groups, vocal choirs at their schools, and church plays over the years of their education. Liisi competed on well-trained cheer and dance teams, and they didn't always win. Sometimes, other teams were just better, even though her team had rehearsed diligently. Her vocal jazz high school group won first place one year when she sang lead one of their competition songs, but not the next. She was chosen as a winner in the Young Arts competition later. Skye got the lead in the church Christmas play, but not the school play, and so it went, the learning of life through these wins and losses.

They both auditioned and got into the prestigious Los Angeles County High School for the Arts or LACHSA which felt like winning the lottery. To attend a school where the arts were deeply nurtured was a perfect fit for them. They were very talented girls, and their hard-wired spirits were leading them into the world of performance arts as well as a world of rejection. How would I teach them that, in show business, sometimes even when you are great, you don't get the job? That there are factors other than talent that sometimes entered into casting decisions?

My children showed an inclination for performing arts from a very young age. They loved performing so much that their dad had a small stage built with purple curtains and drawstrings. If there were more than two people at our home other than us, the girls would announce, "Show in 10 minutes!" and hand out red raffle tickets for performance entry. They would escort you downstairs to the lined up folding green chairs their dad used for his monthly poker games. Our visitors would receive a full-on show without fail, though sometimes they didn't know when to end. It was the thing they loved the most. Skye was always directing, acting, and Liisi was performing five or six of her characters and mimicry. It was so pure and joyful. I loved watching how they grew and how safe they felt to explore artistically in our small basement which was a source of memorable moments and lots of laughter. How would I teach them that even though they were so talented, that success in the business may not come quickly? How even if they'd prepared fully for an audition, it could just be an off day, or they might not be in good singing voice if they had a cold or sinus ailment, or the part might not be well suited to their abilities? And then, when they saw other people getting jobs they knew they could do, how to reconcile that and not become bitter? Or compare their trajectory with others?

It took me back to what my father said to me when I competed in pageants.

At that time, the talent competition weighed a hefty fifty percent of the overall score. I'd shown great interview skills, but in more than fourteen pageants in which I'd won the talent and interview, I didn't win overall. I was always the runner-up. Some of it certainly had to do with the veiled yet obvious racism since I was the only black contestant competing in an all-white pageant, in the South. In those times of disappointment and frustration, I recall what my dad said to me, which I passed along to my girls. He told me, "It's good to win and have it all, but it's also inconvenient because of the pressure it puts on you to always have to win. Some people are only happy as long as they are winning. But it takes a better person to know how to also be a good loser. You have to learn to be happy for those people when they are winning, because when you win in your time, people will be rooting for you. What is for you will be yours. Remember to be as good a loser as you are a winner. That's where the grace is."

In the times when I didn't win, I took solace in having gained the experience and exposure, and a chance to push harder and get better. However, when standing on a stage as someone else's name was called, I had to dig deep to find a genuine smile and sincere congratulations for someone else who had achieved my goal. That's human. But I also learned that not winning doesn't mean "never"; it just means, "not right now." Learning to be a good loser, a gracious loser, was indeed a lesson in grace that Dad gave me and one that helped me grow and toughen my skin.

Recently, our daughter Liisi had an audition for a feature film that would be directed by Denzel Washington. The experience was surreal and would have been a huge career-making vehicle. She rigorously prepared for the role and was at the heady step of the final audition which included a contract for a three-picture deal. Never had she wanted something so much and she felt excited and nervous at the same time. Everyone along the process of three previous auditions had been wonderful to Liisi, the casting office and mostly Mr. Washington. She left her final callback after being in the room with them for an hour and felt that it had gone incredibly well. Then there was the waiting, and we all held our breath with her. After two weeks of waiting, she got the call from her talent team that another young lady had gotten the role and she was devastated. We talked and I reminded her that not everyone gets to be in the room with Denzel or be that close to a breakthrough role. She cried, we cried and held the disappointment together as a family, but knew we had to move on.

About a month later, she learned the name of the talented

actress who landed the role and did something of her own volition that shocked me with joy. She reached out through direct messenger to the actress and explained who she was, that she had been up for the role and that she had never wanted anything so much in her life. But then told her that she was truly happy for her and hoped the role would be a life changing moment in hers. She wished her well. As she read me the text she sent, I wept tears of joy.

She'd got it.

CHAPTER 32

You Can Give Out, But Don't Give Up

My mom once told me that as soon as I could speak, I would throw my head back and sing the vowel sounds with the congregation. In perfect time and tune. She said that when I was three, after Sunday school, while tugging at my dad's coat, I announced that I wanted to sing. I then proceeded to sing the full verse and chorus of *Yes, Jesus Loves Me* while standing on top of the offering table at Mary Evergreen Church. That's the first time my mother saw Dad cry. I've seen people cry when my dad sang. The first voice that sang to me was his. Dad was always singing or humming around the house, at church, when he mowed the lawn, and as he drove us. I watched and learned from hearing him sing with great passion and a deep love of music.

From that point, I sang mostly in church choir and with my sister group, the Whitaker Sisters. Then, beginning when I was eight, I would sing for about five hundred people at the SWEPCO annual Christmas party, the electric and power company where Dad worked evenings. My chosen song? "I Saw Mommy Kissing Santa Claus." Singing was rooted in my family and my dad's voice led the way.

His group, The Spiritual Jubilees, was an all-men gospel group he co-founded with six to eight men. They sang beautiful gospel songs in harmony, slapping their hands to their thighs in rhythm. During their rehearsals, while the other children of these men would run about and play, I'd stay close, listening and learning their harmonies, practicing their different vocal parts. They performed around the Ark-La-Tex area for twenty-one years for large and small churches. My sisters and I would get invited up after the offering during their concerts with an introduction, "I'mma bring my babies up here The Whitaker Sisters, to sing for y'all! Nita, Alene, Kathy and Debbie (my first cousin), y'all come on up!" We'd sing either a couple Clark Sisters songs, or other choir songs of the day in three-part harmony with one of us on lead, usually me. Dad sat with a beaming face from the front pew for his talented family.

So many in my immediate and extended family sang — and sang well — but no one in the circle of my youth pursued it as a way of making a living. It was only a side activity and mostly for church. Singing was something you did for the love of God, and for the love of singing itself. But I had seen enough of the Jackson Five, Diana Ross and the Supremes, along with movie musicals and stars on television to know some people were famous for it and made a living. Could that be possible for me?

I participated in continuous church choirs and musicals in elementary school, then drama club and musicals in high school. At every event, I always listened over the buzz of the audience, the cheers and the noise for my dad's presence. When he cleared his throat, as he often did, that was my signal that he was there. He never missed a performance, whether I was the lead at my first school performance, Mary, Mary Quite Contrary a third-grade operetta (I had a little solo), or in the chorus at Port Players Theater summer day camp in Due To A Lack of Interest, Tomorrow Has Been Cancelled. He and mother sat in my audiences, always beaming with pride and support.

When I was seventeen, during my second semester in college and after my mother died, I signed up for my first beauty pageant: Miss Ebony. I did it as a way of meeting new friends. I knew only one girl, my roommate, and one cousin in the college of ten thousand students. In my hometown, I had been a big fish in a small pond school, as both the homecoming queen and a cheerleader at my high school. College was a lot different, and I missed my friends.

I started "making stuff up", or songwriting, when I was in my teens. For the talent competition at Miss Ebony, I decided I would play and sing one of my original songs. While waiting backstage, I heard Dad's throat-clearing signal, soothing me within. He was there with my siblings and a couple other relatives. When my turn came, I sang my little original song. After the last note, the audience jumped to its feet. I ran off-stage in tears, thinking their reaction meant my performance was horrible, that they had not liked the song, or me.

I had no idea what a standing ovation was, because I'd only known "Holy Ghost" shouting at church, or polite clapping at the annual Christmas parties.

Yet the standing ovation continued. The organizers pushed me back on stage to take another bow. I scanned the audience for my dad's face. I heard his high-pitched whistle first, then the "Woowoowoo!" as my sister Kathy yelled loudly above the crowd. Then I found him, shining, smiling wide-faced so full of pride, witnessing this moment with me.

This was a new feeling…this applause. And I wanted to hear it again.

The next semester, I enrolled in a group singing class, learning basic sight singing and early English songs even though this was not a subject within my nursing major. The instructor, Mr. Louis Nabors, pulled me aside near the end of the semester and said, "Miss Whitaker, I would like to work with you privately, but I want to be careful not to ruin your natural instrument." He said it in a mid-Atlantic accent I found slightly amusing from a 6'6" black-rimmed coke-bottle glasses-wearing black man. For the rest of my college stay, I took private singing lessons from him. He helped me find some parts of my voice that I would not have known, and pushed me to use them.

"I don't want to sing this kind of music. It's too stiff," I told him one day about the classical operatic music and placement he was teaching me, thinking of the rousing gospel music in the churches or the Jackson Five, with their dance moves. All that kind of music felt more fun to perform and I wanted to connect with an audience like I had seen them do; besides, I hadn't quite mastered the foreign languages he had me phonetically singing.

"You will need to know and use this part of your voice, Miss Whitaker," he countered. He then showed me the techniques needed to sing arias, which opened up new sounds in my vocal tones. It also surprised me that I was able to move into such new territory with my voice. With his training, I competed and won a National Association of Teachers (NATS) award for singing an aria from Puccini's Tosca; the private classes and training paid off.

On weekends when I came home from college to play piano for a local church, I would sing some of these new songs for my dad. "That shole is pretty, baby," he said, proud of my new vocal sounds as he beamed with pride. "Keep on goin'."

Following that Miss Ebony pageant, I was invited to participate in another pageant. I figured out quickly, that pageants could give me a stage to sing. For me, they weren't about beauty or having the best body, but about the intellect and the talent— and also earning some money to help pay for school. I entered pageant after pageant because I craved the stage.

After I performed in those competitions, the ovations kept coming. For the first time, I knew singing was what I really wanted to do for my career. By eighteen, the singing seed was deeply planted, gestated in my church groups, nurtured by a wonderful teacher who helped me expand, and watered with love from my dad's and family's ever present support and love. Dad attended every one of those pageants and brought along a caravan of family members, who yelled and cheered wildly, especially during the talent competition. It gave me the confidence to believe that I could sing and make a living doing it.

I continued traveling to small towns throughout northern Louisiana during and after college to compete in these pageants, with my goal of reaching the state level. Most of the girls showed up with their mothers in tow, carrying long garment bags with beautiful gowns and a swimsuit. Since my mother had passed, I traveled alone, but I never felt alone. I knew that my dad, siblings, and some relative would be in the audience at some point, and that was good enough. We could afford one dress, a sky-blue spaghetti strap chiffon dress from Azarue's bridal store in Bossier, Louisiana. I added navy blue rick-rack sequin around the waist to add some sparkle to the plain gown. It was $99, what my dad could afford, and it was long enough to fit my 5'9" slim frame.

I was always the only black girl in these beauty / scholarship pageants, but I didn't think twice about it. I never felt inferior, and I made what turned out to be life-long friendships, because I knew these girls were just like me. The way I saw it, I just came wrapped in beautiful brown packaging, which helped me stand out a bit more. Three amazing women – Georgia Hines, Dixie, and Mary Alice Jackson – mothered me in those pageant days, fed and nurtured me making sure I had the right things that my dear widower dad wouldn't know about. These lovely chaperones quickly became my pageant moms, provided advice, and surrounded me with a spiritual and loving guidance that helped me so much in those early days of pageants. We all loved each other deeply and they helped me grow, especially Mary Alice whom I am still in close contact with and call "Momma".

Fourteen pageants later, I had learned the ways of walking, interviewing and exuding confidence. Still, nothing was more glorious than to get that sweet hug from my dad, whether I won or just placed in all those pageants. I always won the talent portion of the competition, which at that time was 50 percent of the final score. Once, when I placed only second in a pageant, even after winning talent and interview competition, the head of the pageant committee called my father while slightly inebriated telling him, "Mr. Whitaker, she won that pageant, but they couldn't give it to her sir, cause she's black. I'm so sorry! But I just need you to know Anita won that pageant!" he said through booze loosened truth tears. "Well, I knew it, 'cause there wasn't nobody on that stage better than Nita all around," Dad said assuredly. "But I 'preciate you lettin' me know, Mr. Muckleroy."

In between all the pageants, I pursued and obtained my Bachelor of Science degree in nursing, finishing the four-year curriculum in three. Even though there was a zoology teacher in the second semester who failed ninety percent of the class, I worked hard to be in his ten percentile. Failing his class added another semester or two to completion. On a weekend while visiting home, my dad and I were in our backyard on 73rd street when we heard a loud screech, the smell of tires burning on the pavement, and a loud hollow thud of metal colliding between two cars. Being two-thirds through the nursing program and just having finished my neurological rotation, Dad and I ran to the scene to see if we could be of assistance. Just around the corner and down one block from our home, there were two cars entangled, sprawled across the four-lane street, smoke rising from crumpled hoods, part of the cars strewn indiscriminately across the avenue, some people crying and some gathering to look as angry words hung in the air.

I noticed a young black man in the front passenger seat who was barely conscious. A couple people were out of the twisted vehicles, walking about surveying the scene and I went directly to the young man who was obviously in discomfort and was moaning incoherently. I had recently learned not to move someone in that situation unless they were otherwise in danger. His presenting symptoms were, as we say, "textbook" case; his slurred speech, disorientation, a growing goose egg swelling on his forehead were right off the pages. The ambulance had been called and after a quick assessment, I said to my dad who was standing near me, "He has a closed head injury."

I checked his vitals as best I could with no equipment and stayed by his side talking to the young man when the ambulance arrived. The paramedics came and I gave him my quick assessment of what we'd heard and seen. When he assessed the young man and radioed ahead, he also confirmed the patient had a closed head injury. I don't know how many times my dad told family member or people in our church about how I had diagnosed the man at the scene of the accident, saying, "Nita called it before they got there!" He'd always said "Git yo' learnin'" and he was as proud of me in that moment for my intellect as he was when I stood singing on a spotlit stage.

It took four tries for me to win the coveted title of Miss Louisiana. I had practiced Dad's lesson of being a good and gracious loser. By that point, in 1984, the owner of an amazing dress store in Monroe, Frank Massony, had befriended me with great support. He let me have beautiful gowns that were $300 to $400 (a lot of money for a new working nurse). I paid him back as I could, and my pageant wardrobe dramatically improved beyond the blue chiffon bridal gown. In my first two Miss Louisiana pageants, I had won Miss Congeniality, fourth then second runner-up. In my third try, I was the first runner up. Had I won, I would have competed against Vanessa Williams for the 1983

Miss America title. People in my community (but not my home) told me, "Nita, them white folks ain't never gonna let you win!"

I started to believe them. I told my dad that I didn't think Louisiana was gonna let me win and that I should move to Arkansas, where a black girl, Lencola Sullivan, had just won the state title. "Maybe," I said, "they were more open." (Haha! In Arkansas; what was I thinking?)

"I think you should try one more time here, Nita. I got a good feelin' 'bout it," my dad gently told me in his quiet knowing way. In that moment, I reflected on the stories of when he'd worked in the cotton fields, how he worked until exhaustion and got up to do it all again and again for meager wages. His father had taught him that he could give out, but never give up. I knew he spoke from his own journey, from cotton picking days in the unforgiving heat believing in a better way of life. How could I do any less?

I also learned that that sometimes waiting for your door to open could feel exhausting and disappointing, but to get to the win, I had to keep trying. I knew I too would not give up or quit in any area of my life. He had been with me every step from Mary Evergreen Church to this moment of possibly representing my state as the first black girl to do so.

I trusted his words and judgment, entered and won a local pageant called Miss Forest Festival, which put me back at the Miss Louisiana pageant for the fourth time. My dad prayed with me and said, "Just go out there and do your best. You can win this."

A few days later, I stood on stage and heard the announcement: "And our new Miss Louisiana is… Contestant #33 Anita Whitaker!"

As the rhinestone crown was placed atop my coiffed head, I scanned the convention auditorium for my dad; felt sure his face was wet with tears as was mine. You were right, Daddy, I thought as I stood before the standing crowd, trying to take in the moment. Yes, there had been times I had thought of quitting, but I persisted. My mother had dreamed of a moment like this for me and Dad's faith in my ability to win the title never wavered, and he showed up every time to show me that.

Overjoyed and newly crowned me,
Miss Louisiana with then Governor Edwin Edwards

CHAPTER 33
Beware Of Wolves In Sheep's Clothing

It was time for me to leave Shreveport, the place I had lived in, loved, and known. Home. I was in my twenties and felt a calling to try new adventures and avenues.

Dad understood I wanted to grow more in my singing career, but he was understandably concerned. I was moving eighteen hundred miles away to California, and he must have felt what I later felt when my daughters left for college, hoping he had taught me enough life skills to help me survive what he believed was the wild world of show business. He hoped he had taught me enough. We've all heard the many stories of casting couches and girls getting duped into compromising situations in the pursuit of their careers. He had been worried when I took myself to New York for a vacation to see my first Broadway show, because on television it was portrayed as a crazy place with all manner of unruly crimes and evil intentions, "the devil's den," as he thought of it. I went anyway and had an extraordinary time, for which he was genuinely thrilled. He had faith in my ability to fulfill my dreams.

I packed my light yellow 190E Mercedes with everything I owned to start my new journey in California. The compact car bulged at the seams with all my gowns, shoes, street clothes, church clothes, some bedding, a television set, nurse scrubs, and accessories for ICU nursing work that awaited me—all the things that would help me transition. I was prepared to take the leap and head west to chase my dream of singing for the world while nursing on the side to pay the way. Both nervous and excited, I wanted to make a name for myself outside of my small town.

I was the first in my immediate family to fly the coop and head so far west. The week before I planned to leave, while I was collecting and packing up, Daddy had so much to tell me. He was beside himself as we loaded the last things into my nearly packed car. My cousin Diane, who lived in California, had agreed to be my companion for the trip. Dad was talking non-stop, giving me many verbal gems to carry on my way. Usually he said just a few words, or a sentence or two to deliver his point, but that early morning he squeezed in a few more—words to think about and incorporate into my consciousness to keep me safe, remind me of common sense smarts, and act like an empowered woman.

"Don't put yourself in harm's way," he reminded me. He wanted me to think about choices that held potential harm in them. "Travel in well-lit areas," he added, and "always let someone know where you are." He continued, "And if you go to a party and put your drink down, just go get another one. Don't ever drink anything someone gives you that you didn't see them make." He had heard a story about a young man in our neighborhood who drank something someone gave him, and was never quite the same.

As we continued loading, Dad gave me another pearl of his wisdom, "Everybody's not gonna have your standards, but you don't stoop to theirs, you make them rise to yours." "I'll remember these, Daddy," I assured him. I acknowledged all the things he said wanting him to know that I really listened and heeded his wise advice.

As I sat in the driver's seat of the car, nearly ready to pull out of the carport, Dad offered me one final gem: "And one more thing Nita, beware of wolves in sheep's clothing. See, there are people who will cozy up and try to get in your circle when really they are trying to get what you got." He reminded me that not everyone was out to get me, but to "keep a sharp eye" for signs of that kind of person. He then added, "Everyone is not there for your benefit, and everybody can't be your best friend. So, don't trust everybody right away. They can look one way and be another. Be smart and watch and wait." I tucked all these nuggets into the storeroom of my memory to retrieve as necessary, but those pearls all created a luster within me as I readied myself to head away from a loving world in which I was known.

I have been lucky in my career, as both a nurse and a singer, to meet some good and decent people, musicians and other artistic friends who opened their hearts and some doors to help me achieve some of my dreams of sharing my singing with the world. That's why I moved. Still, there were moments that could have gone another way if I hadn't had his advice in my head. Once there was a producer I was working with who walked up behind me, put his arm around my waist and commented that I wasn't wearing a bra. My reply was, "Why are you looking?" and that was the end of that. I've been invited to "prayer meetings" which I had never heard of. It is drinking shots of tequila and praying you made it back to your room. I always declined and went to my room with just a soda. I was a nerd that way but I didn't care nor did I want to, as Daddy said, put myself in harm's way.

I wanted to be near the industry that called me, and I've created an incredible village in the pursuit of those dreams. It hasn't always been the easiest, and certainly as with most artists, not a straight road. I've had some setbacks and disappointments along with the triumphs. There are still dreams for me to dream. But I wanted to sing and that is what I do, even with some wolves lurking, I gained a life more amazing than Shreveport ever could have afforded me. And when I discovered those wolf/sheep people as instructed, I gently weeded them out.

As my daughters began to walk into their artistic lives, I shared some of my dad's pearls with them in hopes it could help them be a little smarter with some of their decisions and help them stay a little safer. I guess I must've shared these many times because when I repeat it now, they remind me, "Mom, you've told us this!"

With a smile I say, "I'm sure I have, but some things bear repeating."

CHAPTER 34
In Every Ovation

After representing my state as Miss Louisiana, and then competing for the title of Miss America, the time of pageants was over for me. My goal at that time had been to be chosen as a top ten contestant, which would have given me the opportunity to perform on national television. Disappointingly, that did not happen, not even a talent win, and I now knew I had to find another way in; pound the pavement as others had done and find a way to get me closer to my dreams of singing.

Star Search was another test in perseverance, for which my dad was my biggest support and my keep-going guru. I traveled to auditions for the wildly popular competition television show in hopes of getting a spot. I went to Nashville, Houston, and twice to Dallas. After waiting in a long line, each singer walked into a room with a camera, a cameraman and strong lights, and sang to some invisible people in a control booth. Usually I sang a couple of songs with a music track or acapella, and I wondered how the judges would be able to really hear all our songs but like the other singers, I hoped my audition songs could break through and earn me a spot on the show. Later, I learned that if you got a letter, that usually meant you didn't get in. The letters always began with, "Although we enjoyed your audition, regretfully…" and I received four such letters. However, in my quest for stages, I competed and won the "Tomorrowland Girl of Beauty" a competition that was talent based, and received a short-lived modeling contract.

I auditioned and won a spot on two television competition shows in Los Angeles, Miss Hollywood, produced by ABC and Dick Clark's company, and Dreamgirls USA, a weekly televised talent competition show. I was confident that the years of pageants had prepared me for these upcoming competitions. No one was more excited than my dad.

Off I went into another new world of made-for-television events, and met a couple of people who would change the direction of my life, Jeff Margolis and Lee Miller.

We rehearsed dance numbers, filmed vignettes on location, and practiced parts of the show with the other contestants. All of it was enchanting to me and I fell more in love with performing. The talented artistic contestants varied in art forms from opera to pop singing, ballet to jazz dancing, and comedic to dramatic acting. We stayed at the Universal Hilton Hotel, two girls to a room. Alan Thicke was the host for the live broadcast. During the show, the top ten contestants had a live screen test with a handsome actor from the show "Dynasty". We also had an interview, talent competition, and a celebrity panel of judges to choose the best overall "It" factor.

I learned so much about the production process and filming scenes. After that heady two-week experience, I was truly bitten by the showbiz bug.

Jerry Seinfeld performed between the girls' routines and interviews for the televised show. He was sweet on my roommate and, always a gentleman, we said a few hellos those times he came by our room. I called my dad and told him about this funny young comedian hitting on my roommate. His routine on that show had been about the use of cotton balls. It was brilliant; he later used it on a segment of his hit television show, "Seinfeld"!

I told him about all the sites we visited—Arturo's Florist, Patty's Diner, Venice Beach, Universal Studios—all which we'd filmed for the show, and my first taste of sushi, rice and raw fish. He could not for the life of him understand why they wouldn't want to fry it.

Two hundred friends and family members were in the Los Angeles audience when we taped the show, and they went crazy with cheers after I performed "New York, New York." I adored the applause. The director and assistant director, Jeff Margolis and Lee Miller (who both went on to have illustrious producing and directing careers), sat me down and encouraged me to get out of Shreveport where I had established a successful nursing career and give my big singing dreams a try. Jeff said to me, "We really think you should give it a try, this singing. You should move to Los Angeles; you can always go back to nursing if it doesn't work out, but if you don't try you won't ever know."

Why they singled me out, I will never know, but it was just the push I needed.

I placed second runner-up on that show with a five-thousand-dollar cash prize which turned into no money but a trip to Fiji, which got cancelled because of a military coup, which became my first Caribbean cruise on a small Italian cruise ship with very fragrant waiters, but also was my first real taste of show business outside of the pageant world, I wanted more. I knew I had to try.

The wrap party was at the famed Hollywood Roosevelt Hotel. As I was walking in, a very tall, dark-skinned man with big bright teeth and kind eyes stopped me in the lobby. "I sure enjoyed your singing tonight." We struck up a conversation. He was dressed in a black suit with a hot pink shirt matching pocket square, shiny black-pointed toe shoes. He looked quite dapper. His name was Tony Warren; we became fast and best friends. We learned we were both Southerners and knew the same kind of old school church music. Later that summer, I invited him to Shreveport to sing at my church. He came and tore the church up! Tony had moved to Los Angeles four years before to pursue his career. He was an incredible singer whose range could reach the high tones of Aretha Franklin while dropping as low and silky as Barry White. He also knew that I belonged in Los Angeles if I wanted to advance my singing career.

I was working full time in an intensive care unit in Shreveport and would take time off to try to sing here and there to advance my career, but those words, along with my dad's blessing and love helped me make the move toward my bigger dreams. When I looked back I realized that every musical endeavor, whether church or pageant or school was a part of my musical schooling journey; there are no mistakes and everything, whether a win or a loss, comes to teach us.

I am so blessed that I don't know a time that my dad wasn't there to support me for all the big and small moments of my life.

How many girls can say that? The words he and Mother planted in me through their doings, sayings, and living were a well of riches from which I could draw. Whatever stage I stand on today, my dad is right there with me. The bag full of gems he gave to help me trust my gifts and know my worth and to go for my dreams is packed into every performance, every interaction, and in every ovation. His angel prayers and guidance have traveled with me, and the rest as they say, is my history.

CHAPTER 35
For Two Or Two Thousand

———◆———

I arrived in Los Angeles, eager to make my mark as a singer and, with a traveling nurse job to support me, I came with an excited heart and bigger dreams. The string of wins I'd accumulated before making the decision to move had bolstered my confidence.

After I moved to LA, Tony Warren began to introduce me to his friends and fans. I was holding down a full-time job at Brotman Medical Center, working three to four twelve-hour shifts per week in their medical intensive care, where I took care of open-heart surgery and neurological patients. On my off days, I'd go with Tony to different clubs and restaurants around town and he delighted in his introduction of me as his new friend—a Miss Louisiana pageant-winning friend who was "the first black, and who sings better than Whitney Houston!" No pressure.

When I met him, Tony had developed quite a fan following, and had won a local singing competition at a club called "The Rose Tattoo". I picked him up one day and he took me to meet the owner. Tony went on and on about me and my talents almost to my embarrassment. With no big credits other than my Miss Louisiana crown, the Miss America performance, the televised Miss Hollywood and Dreamgirls USA performances, and a couple performances in a Las Vegas lounge, Mr. Ed Tourgaman, an olive-skinned, black-haired man with a business demeanor and a prominent black moustache, was impressed enough to give me a spot on his ongoing singing competition called Stardom Pursuit. It was at The Rose Tattoo's performances that I met my other Los Angeles friends for life, Adam Jackson Jr., Will Wheaton, and one I would marry, Don LaFontaine. There were many fine people riding the same train with us, all pursuing our artistic goals and dreams.

I called my dad and shared these new experiences, telling him who I'd met and how exciting it all felt. I loved sharing all the things I was experiencing and to hear his genuine excitement for me.

There wasn't a road map to how I would begin, but I had Tony. I will always love him for being my angel guide when I landed in L.A. When he performed in his cabaret shows around town, I would go to support him and to learn by watching what he did. He introduced me to his audience by passing me a microphone so I could sing a part of one of the songs in his set. His singing was precise and raw: precise in pitch, raw in his ability to throw a church riff with a new vocal run that never occurred to me. He was thrilling to witness: supremely talented, quick witted and outrageously funny. If I sang too well, he'd snatch the mic back and the audience would roar with laughter. He'd even passed it around to different singers within the room. All of this helped to build my self-esteem in my new town. It made me feel like I was finding my place . . . a bit.

I had come from a pageant audience, where if you sang a high, long, or loud note, they applauded like you were Whitney Houston or Barbara Streisand. Because of that, my audience meter was skewed. In Louisiana, I was a big fish in a small pond, but my insatiable quest to be witnessed by bigger audiences drove me to move on. It was time, after a year and half of introductions and singing sometimes at The Rose Tattoo, to do my own cabaret show at one of the places where Tony had introduced me—the famed Gardenia Room. It was small, only able to hold sixty people, but I was sure I could fill it. I had flyers printed and mailed to my large handfuls of cousins, aunts, uncles, and people I had met since coming to the city.

It happened on a frigid mid-February night, one of the coldest nights on record in L.A. at the time. I was there with my backing trio (piano, bass, and drums), prepared to do a set of ten-plus songs for my adoring audience. I had been there for Tony's shows, and it was always packed and full of anticipation for how and what he would do and sing.

It was nearing show time. At 7:55 p.m., the club manager came back to give me a five-minute heads up. We held the room for twelve minutes past the 8 p.m. downbeat, which simply meant we started late, hoping some late guests would mosey in. I walked out for my opening number wearing one of the glittering sequined gowns from my pageant days. My band played the opening number while I walked down the wide aisle looking long and lean. A spotlight was shining on me as I moved to the apex of the supper club so I was blinded from seeing the room. When I turned around to take in my audience, there were nine people in the place. Their sparse but cheerful applause was swallowed up by the hollowness of the nearly empty room and the sound of the trio playing. I was stunned. I had never not had a full audience. I'd won countless talent contests, competed for freaking Miss America, and only nine people showed up? My ego was wounded.

One of my worst performances followed. My head was definitely not in the game — or on the tiny stage in that small room. Self-doubt walked up and slapped me in the throat, filling my mind with negative thoughts like, "You're really not that good", and "People don't really want to hear you sing." I was so thrown by this low turnout that I began to doubt my talents, and on the verge of tears for the first two or three songs. It affected my voice, which trembled not with vibrato but raw emotion. As the singers say, "It took my throat."

It felt like a rejection in that room, in my new town that I so desperately wanted to embrace me. I got through it somehow, but afterwards, I felt equally let down inside for having delivered a lackluster performance.

I was quiet on the ride home. My then-boyfriend, Don, who had seen me sing many times to seemingly wowed crowds in Los Angeles supper clubs, was kind in his comments. When I said, "That was just awful . . .and nobody came," he just said, "Well, honey, it wasn't your best." Always honest, just enough of the sweet and the salty.

When I got home, I immediately called my dad, though it was late for him. I told him about the near empty club, how nobody came, that I didn't sing well, and how upset I was about everything. I asked him how he could sing at churches when people didn't show up or the crowds were skimpy.

He said simply, "Well, baby, you do the same show for two as you would for two thousand. Those people who came wanted to hear you sing and they deserve the best of what you have to give. You never know who you are reaching and how you may be affecting their lives. Always give your best, even if no one or only two are watching."

Fast forward to the arena in Mexico City, Mexico holding forty thousand screaming fans…

I stood next to Andrea Bocelli as we sang one of our duets, Somos Novios. This was preceded by chanting cheers in the arena when the native Mexican songwriter Armando Manzenaro, who wrote the song, walked ahead to accompany us on piano. I looked out from an incredible stage filled with a full orchestra dressed in black, into an abyss of faceless fans, cheers, camera flashes and spotlights with Steven Mecurio conducting the orchestra. This was what I had dreamed of. Still, even in that amazing moment, I didn't feel that far away from that younger Nita who played to her meager audience of nine. It was another great lesson in humility and grace.

I felt warmed as the spotlight bathed me in her light and overwhelmed in this mountain top moment, this musical dreamed-for-moment. Wearing a flaming red Badgley Mischka gown, hair flowing, I stood center stage sharing the spotlight with Andrea and his voice harmonizing with mine. I knew I had to get those Spanish lyrics right, because of where we were; I'd rehearsed ad nauseum to be my best. My dad's words rang in my ears as our voices, Andrea's and mine, blended in the "popera" duet. Mexico City could not get enough of us.

I escorted Andrea on my arm for a staged encore. We waited less than thirty seconds as the crowd robustly and loudly cheered, stomped and chanted for his return. "Bravo Bravo!!" and "Una Mas!!" The roar was a tidal wave wall of sound as we came back onto the stage. We sang the second duet, "The Prayer", and you could hear a pin fall, followed by a thunderous eruption of cheers. It was a sound and a feeling I will cherish and never forget.

"For two or two thousand… always give you best," Dad had said. Or forty thousand. Those words stuck like hot grits.

CHAPTER 36
Stick Together

———◆———

There are words that stick long after they are said, that come around
to another generation with meaning that reverberates just as much as
they did when first spoken.

When my dad was growing up, the Whitaker boys and girls
understood that they were always to travel in pairs. This basic rule of
comings and goings, given by their father, was a means of protection
and support during the times in which they lived. But it also held
a deeper meaning. Their dad was a wise, kind father, and at heart a
teacher with a bright loving spirit.

One evening after field and home chores were done, Poppa Isaac
gathered the children and sat them down. He passed several short
brown twigs around as the kids looked around, bewildered. First, he
asked them if they could break the sticks; those with the small sticks
did so with minimal effort. Next, he pulled out sets of twigs that he
had bound together with twine and asked them to see if they could
break those. They could not. He then said to them, "Chil'ren, this is
why we travel together, eat together, and love together. Like these
sticks show, that if you stick together, you are stronger. Now, remember that."

After my daughters' eighth- and twelfth-grade graduations, we
held a gathering at our Los Angeles home. My dad had flown to L.A.
from Louisiana many times to witness everything from their baptisms
to their elementary school graduations and other milestone achievements; he was present for this occasion as well. As we sat around the
dinner table, the day nearly done, I asked everyone assembled to share
some wise words for the girls to carry with them.

It was extremely important to have this family and village
support for my daughters, because their sweet father had died at
the beginning of that school year. They would not have his voice and

wisdom present, though his love drummed in their hearts. That enormous loss created a surreal year, and I was trying to be both mother and father. And I was concerned about how they were grieving, since children grieve differently. I thought they could absorb some wise words from trusted family and friends. Some gave dating advice (to the soon-to-college one), some spoke about how to navigate high school or how to choose friends from others. Some gave favorite quotes or Bible verses, the conversation lively and interactive.

Finally, my dad spoke. "I wanna share something with you that my Poppa taught me."

He pulled out some twigs from inside his front shirt pocket and asked the girls to break them. Of course they were perplexed, with no idea where this story was going or what he was trying to do or say. They knew he was about to show them something important, though. Then he pulled out another set of brown twigs bound by twine and asked them to try to break it. They could not.

"My daddy showed me this when I was a boy," Dad said. "Now, Skye, you going off to college and Liisi, you headed to a new high school. You not gonna be together like you were before as a family, but you are getting yo' learning and that's a good thing you must do. But no matter where you go in life, you and yo' sister stick together. Stand up for one another and don't let anyone break your bond. Ain't but the two of you who got the same blood in yo' veins, and family is greater than any bond you will ever have. So as you move around your lives, you girls always remember to stick together, love each other, stay together, and be there for one another. You are better and stronger together, just like these bonded sticks."

After a big, collective sigh, there was nothing more to be said. My dad's words hung in the air like the fragrance of a fresh gardenia blossom, then landed on our hearts.

CHAPTER 37

Be An Ant, Not A Grasshopper

My youngest nephew, Jamerrio, was visiting me in California for a weekend. During our visit, Jamerrio shared how Dad, his grandfather, was continuing to tell stories of his life with the next generation of our family. He told me that while visiting home from McNeese University, where he was an All-Conference defensive end, he drove home to Shreveport and upon arrival noticed my dad wiping down his car with a clean worn towel. Jamerrio parked in the driveway and quizzically asked, "Poppa, whatcha doing?"

Dad replied, "I'm keeping this car clean, that's all. A little bit every day so it don't get so dirty. You know, son, you gotta be like an ant, not like a grasshopper."

Slightly amused, and knowing he was in for a good story, Jamerrio asked what he meant.

"You see son, the story goes there was a grasshopper who loved to chirp loudly and hop around on the bright summer days. He saw an ant walking by, grunting under the weight of a fat white kernel of corn. You know they can carry ten times their size, right? The grasshopper asked him where he was going with that heavy thing. Without stopping, the ant said, 'To our ant hill. It's my fourth trip today.' 'Well, why don't cha stop, come and sing and play with me instead of workin' so hard?' the grasshopper asked him.

"I am storing up some food for the winter and think you oughta do the same," the ant said.

"'Why you worry 'bout winter now? Look how nice the day is. Worry 'bout winter when winter come,' said the grasshopper. 'There is plenty of food and fun right now!' Then he hopped on away thinkin' the ant would follow him. But that ant kept on workin' and kept on walkin'.

"And when the weather turned cold, and sleet and snow covered the ground, that 'ole grasshopper couldn't find no food, so he didn't feel like hoppin' and jumpin' and found himself nearly dying of hunger. Then he stumbled to the ant's hill and saw the ants handing out the corn to feast on from the summer's stockin' up. That was when he got it, that it is better to prepare for those rainy cold days instead of waiting 'til the cold days show up.

"You see, son," my dad continued, "the ant works through the good times to prepare for when they ain't. And we all gonna have 'em. Don't spend everything you make! And try to save at least a dime out of every dollar, more if you can, especially when you are young, healthy, with lots of vitality, and times are good."

My nephew smiled, understanding the story, "Thanks, Poppa!" he said. "Love that!" loving the story, the lesson, and appreciating the storyteller.

When Jamerrio shared that with me, I remembered how Mom and Dad had saved to get ahead, and how he always believed in storing up, the way his mother had stored canned foods preparing for winter season. "Winter," Dad said, "Can be a sickness, or a time of no work, or just a really rough patch," he explained. "The moral of the story is that it is important to be smart and save now while you're young and spry, and full of energy... be like that ant, or you'll find yourself a day late and a dollar short like that hard-headed grasshopper."

CHAPTER 38
It's Just A Season
———

I never know how the conversations will go when I call my dad. Sometimes I've called just to say, "I love you", while other times, he will call to check on us. I'll ask him about something going haywire with my car, discuss a work issue at my home, to share what's going on in my world or his, or get his parenting counsel, and he always has something brilliant and sometimes silly to add.

Our chats usually start like this: "Hey Poppee, how are you today?"

He always says, "Hey, baby girl, I'm fair to middling! How you?"

If I say, "Hey, Dad, whatcha up to?" his reply will be, "Oh 'bout six foot, two!"

And then we're off! Makes me giggle every time. I've called him to talk me off the ledge about a situation or two as well. He always says just the right thing. Maybe I'll get a story or a lesson or just a good "heart talk" with my dad. Whatever and whenever, our lively conversations are always a delight.

Our lives have been further enriched by all the time he's spent visiting us in California. My village here has grown to know and love him, too. Once he performed a concert at my church as a fundraiser after we recorded his first solo gospel record. In our conversations, he often asks how people in our village are doing, and we talk about the weather in our respective places, or what my brother was up to. Always, he asks about the girls. They have cultivated a very sweet loving relationship with their Poppa, their only living biological grandparent. They both have long conversations with him, and I look forward to our phone calls because he has never failed to say something that makes me think, cracks me up, or calms me down.

As we began the conversation one day, I was walking to my car from a meeting. My dad's "lady friend", Ms. Angie Hadnot, has been a lovely companion for him for the past ten years. She, too, was widowed and lived in a small town twenty miles away. She helps her daughter in her seasonal tax business. Dad and Ms. Angie had been seeing each other a couple of years when Dad told me of a conversation they had, where she expressed her frustration at not being able to see or visit with him as much during tax season. He told her, "Listen, I'm gon' be here. Your daughter needs you to help her right now, so you be there for her."

"But my time with you is important and I miss us getting to be together," she continued. To that he replied, "You are helping her so much and you don't have to worry about me. It's just a season."

His words really struck me. I asked him to repeat it. He said again, "It's just a season, just like life."

Instead of driving, I turned off the engine and parallel parked on the street. He expounded: "There is a time and season to everything. And like the days we worked in the fields, I learned there is a time to plant and a time to harvest. God has shown us that there are also seasons in our lives reflected in the seasons of the earth. Sometimes it's sunny and warm like a lovely summer day, and sometimes it's cold, dark and rainy like the bleakest winter nights. Life is full of some real good days and bad ones too. The Bible taught us that there are seasons of storms in our lives. You're either going into one, in the midst of one, or coming out of one. But if we can remember that the situation did not come to stay, it comes to pass, and in the passing of that season we grow stronger in our faith, then we can forge on knowing that change is on the way." He finished with, "Naw, it didn't come here to stay. It come to pass, just like a season."

I knew Daddy preached a sermon just right for me at that moment. Hallelujah and Amen!

CHAPTER 39

Love 'Em With A Long-Handled Spoon

I love sharing with my dad the daily routines of my life, my friendships, and all the things about making a life and family. We always have great exchanges. He has "learned" me as his adult child, and I have learned more about him as a man and not just my father. Dad and I both have a large capacity for empathy, and I was content with that for a time, but he warned me that some people would take my kindness as a weakness and try to use me. I could not imagine that happening, but after it did a few times I was the wiser for it. Some lessons are best learned from experience.

There were some people we both experienced in our lives that had to get weeded out from the close circle. Those in our close circles innately know that friendships are a two-way street; the give and take between us can replenish one another and the support is always unconditional. Dad would say to me, "Be smart, not everybody is happy for you, but you can be happy for them. And there are just some people that will suck the life out of you if you let them."

He and I both have open spirits. For me, being born in the South, that need-to-please gene was nurtured and rewarded as part of the "good girl" selfless way. My dad believed that most people carried goodness in them, but he warned that sometimes people can just "wear you out." Even people in your family, who always need you for something, can pull from you any way they can. Dad always said that "life is the greatest teacher so when you learn the lesson, don't forget it."

I was talking with Dad one day about a certain friend who always needed a lot of emotional support. Whenever I left her, I was totally depleted. There seemed never to be enough that I could do, or listen long enough, or understand deep enough, even though a lot of what she was going through was of her own making and the consistent bad choices she made. She was going to be one of those people, I learned, that though nice in her own way, would always have heaps of problems and loads of upheaval and needed someone to dump it on. At some point, I realized I didn't want to be someone's trash can, doormat, or ATM. About those kinds of people, Dad said, "You just love 'em with a long-handled spoon."

What I finally learned, after trusting myself to be able to recognize certain traits in people who were emotional vacuums, or constantly needed bailouts (financial or otherwise), was that they didn't have to be in the nucleus of my life. They could stay on the periphery, not because they were bad people, but because the drain, emotional or otherwise, pulled too much away from and out of me. I was not willing to give that much of myself away if it wasn't to my immediate family and closest friends.

Dad reminded me that most everybody is special to someone. As for the ones that constantly need something from you, drain you with their constant emotional upheavals and inevitably annoy you? Dad says, "We don't throw them out. Just love 'em from a distance."

CHAPTER 40
I'm Gon' Be As Lazy As I Been Smart

My dad has never shied away from work or an opportunity to get ahead by working harder. I don't recall a day that he didn't work, except after he sprained his back catching a kid in a wheelchair from rolling off the lift on his bus. Among his many jobs, Dad was a co-owner of a local funeral home named Good Samaritan for ten years. And added to that, he and Mom welcomed some of my aunts into our home on their way through college, helped with some of their expenses when they could, all while working and raising the four of us.

For thirty-five years, he drove a school bus rising early each morning. Though this was his source of steady income, I remember him almost always being in motion: driving, walking, mowing, meeting, collecting, and "churching." Daddy says, "I think if you enjoy what you do, then you don't stop doing it; that keeps you going, to feel like you doing something to connect to life instead of sitting around looking ugly at the TV."

I recall his school bus mornings began around 6 AM and most of his days ended at 9:30 p.m. He'd come home tired, but would find the energy for hugs and maybe a piggyback ride but never before he gave our mother a sweet kiss. Working nights at the power company, "sleep would fall on him," he said, so he'd take a quick nap in one of the stalls with the broom propped against the entry door. He had another mop in the stall with him and when he heard it fall, that meant someone had come in, so he'd grab his mop, jump up quickly, and get back to working, straight out of a dead sleep. It was a survival mode technique that he used to get through some of the most exhausting nights. Dad never complained about all the work for all the years, or the kind of work. He made friends where he went, delighted in doing a good job, and just worked.

He didn't stop working, even after retiring from driving the school bus, because he still enjoyed being engaged with people. His side hustle, insurance debt collecting for life and burial policies, had begun years before and was going strong. Since he gains a lot of joy from social and personal connections, Dad chatted with families and became trusted and beloved by his insured. For a while, he was the top debit insurance salesman in the state, for which he won many travel prizes, including trips to Vegas, Canada, and Beijing. He enjoyed them all. My dad has always been open to learning new things and experiences, another quality we share.

Daddy was chairman of the deacon board and the finance committee at his church through his seventies, joined the foster grandparent's association in his eighties, modeled in a fashion show at ninety, and performed at local churches in a musical in the role of Jesus. His schedule included Bible study every Wednesday night and the gym most Mondays and Thursdays. When his brother Dave came to live with him eight years ago, they'd stay up until one in the morning playing dominoes and talking smack to each other with code words from their youth. It was still a full life for a ninety-five-year-old, though it is a different kind of full now. He still enjoys church commitments, watches old westerns, Perry Mason and Family Feud with a passion and still watches his favorite soap, General Hospital.

I love seeing him sleep in now most mornings when I go back home to Louisiana. He says the best part of these days is not having to get up so early. "You gotta fight to be here," he explains. "Keep your body moving, but right now, I'm gon' be as lazy as I been smart."

He's been really smart, and I am thrilled he can enjoy this lazy time to just be and not just be as busy.

CHAPTER 41
We Walk By Faith

While visiting with my dad in Shreveport, we ended one night with a quick kitchen chat after dinner. My flight was leaving early the next morning, and I didn't want to wake him for a "so-long" hug before leaving. Daddy had run some errands earlier in the day and had gone to the gym to work out. My sweetheart Scott and I had cleaned, nested, and cooked meals for my dad, brother, and uncle for the week.

Before dinner, we had all watched a couple episodes of Family Feud with Steve Harvey on the big-screen TV on a loop, trying to guess out loud what the survey would say. After a dinner of homemade red beans and rice, roasted chicken, cornbread, and turnip greens, we relaxed a while. Dad wore his usual clothes from his day, a short-sleeve three-button cotton shirt, with a pocket on the left for his pens. His trousers were still belted at the waist, but the shirt was untucked and he was wearing burgundy cloth house slippers and socks for foot warmth and comfort. Scott and I had on jeans, tee shirts and, as we all slowly got quieter, we decided it was time to end the day.

In the kitchen, I hugged him and said, "I can never hug you enough, Daddy." I always want him to know how much I love and adore him and what a wonderful father he has been. He has a way of making each of his children feel singularly special to him.

"I love you, sweet baby girl," he said.

I hugged him again. "I'm so happy I get to be your baby girl."

He smiled at me with that same dimpled right cheek I have always loved. He continued, "You know, we can't see everything we want, but we walk by faith."

I felt a story coming on and propped myself against the countertop across from dad but next to Scott. "That's right, Daddy, you taught me that."

"There was a little boy," he started, "and his daddy had given him a kite and a spool of thread to play with one day. He went out to a big field and he attached the kite. The wind took it way above the clouds so that only the faint string of thread could be seen. A man walking by looked up and, not seeing anything, shrugged. Later he came by again, and the little boy was still standing there and seemed to be holding just an empty spool.

"Looking up, the man asked the boy why he was holding the spool of thread attached to nothing. The boy replied, 'I'm flying a kite.' The man said, 'But you can't see it, how do you know it's there?' The boy replied, 'I feel it tug a little every now and then.'"

Dad paused for a moment, then went on. "You see, God is like that; we can't see Him, but we know that He is there. We can feel Him every now and then, in the winds, in the great movements of the ocean, and in the majesty of the great mountains and trees, and in the love of a family."

"Wow," I said, "that's a beautiful story, Dad."

"It's just the truth," he replied confidently.

With a nod and a sweet wink, Dad went to his bedroom, and Scott and I headed to the guest room, filled up with good food, sweet family, and wise words.

CHAPTER 42
Eighty Acres

Recently I visited my ancestral land, the eighty acres that my grand-father bought and owned in the early part of the last century. I never knew my grandfather because he died in 1944, but my dad always shared stories of him. We drove down to the small town of Holly, a forty-five-minute drive from Dad's home in Shreveport. Surprising-ly, it was only about twenty-five minutes further than Frierson and Gayles, where we went to church on Sundays when I was a kid. Why we never before went to Holly, to this place, I am not sure but it had been the community and home that held so many warm, wild and wonderful memories for him. I asked Dad why he had not taken us to Holly. My brother remembered going before and his reply was, "We was busy living." I believe there was some pain attached to that sweet place that was taken from them and who wants to revisit old pain?

As we drove down the wide, two-lane black top road, we passed the church where most of the Whitaker family attended and are now buried. I'd visited both the church and the cemetery in the past, for services and funerals of family members.

"Holly," a green metal road sign announced. Just past the sign was another road. We turned right, with Dad directing me, recalling the way. As we came to Firestone Road, he said, "Here is our road, turn right."

As I rounded the corner, he told me that the long road was made of gravel when he was a boy, and he and his family walked it many times to get to church. "Dad's property started right here," he said. "All this was cultivated." It was at the apex of the road, where wild grasses lined the black top road on either side, with forested land beyond that stretched as far as we could see down the unlined asphalt road.

"All this was our land," Dad said as we drove for what felt like a mile. "All the way to the trees." We passed spaced-out simple homes and occasionally stubby steel oil or gas machinery as we continued down the road until we came upon a sweet, sun-yellow house set in a grassy clearing. "And our house was right here," Dad said.

At that point, I felt the need to walk this part of the land, to feel connected to the earth on which my grandfather and father walked, played, ran, worked and lived. I carried my smartphone so that I could capture some video and pictures because it was new to me, though I'd heard about the eighty acres since my earliest years. When I thought about how Poppa Isaac worked to buy that land, he had had to be quite an exceptional planner. It was not easy to be a black landowner in early twentieth century Louisiana. There were a few others who also owned their land, but it was a small minority in the Louisiana south.

I put the car in park and stood on the edge of the grassy lawn. I waved toward the house to attract the attention of whoever was there, so they would see that I was friendly. "Girl, you gonna get us shot!" my sister Kathy said. But I knew I had to touch the land, put my feet there. As I paced the perimeter edge where the grass met the road, I felt the emotion welling up inside me and a great pride in the grandfather that I never knew, pride that this land was where he raised his family of nineteen, pride in their ability to be self-sufficient.

Just then I noticed a Caucasian gentleman standing on the front porch of the house. I waved toward him and spoke despite the distance between us. "You might want to get your behind back in this car," my sister said, but instead, I stood and made eye contact with him. I wanted to know if he knew the land's history before it got to his family. Since we were in the pandemic, I kept my distance, not bringing a mask because I didn't think I would see anyone.

"Hello! My name is Nita. My grandfather owned this land," I yelled.

The balding, medium-height man had a little pot belly and black-rimmed reading glasses hanging around his neck of his white tee shirt, his hands tucked halfway into the pockets of his loose knee-length jean shorts. "This land has been in my family since the 1930s," he replied.

"Yes, it was bought from my grandfather," I said.

I waited for a response, not knowing what to expect. What if he thought I was a trespasser?

He then asked, "What's your name?"

"Whitaker!" I yelled back.

He nodded slightly and began to walk in my direction, always keeping a respectfully safe COVID-19 distance.

He approached as my dad, sister and brother sat with the windows rolled down in Dad's car, witnessing this new interaction. With his fingertips still in his pocket, the man confirmed everything I had been told — except who came before him.

"My name is Johnny Hoell, H.O.E.L.L.," he said with a thick southern drawl. "My mother bought this property in the 30s."

"She bought it from my grandfather Isaac," I said, feeling quite proud.

"She died in 1974, and me and my two brothers inherited the eighty acres," he continued. "I ended up with this section here." He motioned to the plot of land on which we were both standing. "My two brothers sold their parts and I stayed here. Cain't leave," he sheepishly told me.

"I understand," I said.

"The old house they had that was here was still here."

"Wow…" I said aloud. If I had known about this earlier, or if my dad had thought of it, I could have seen the original home.

"We tore that house down thirty years ago and I built this house about twelve years ago," the man continued, filling me in. I felt amazed and overwhelmed at all this information and confirmation. He went on to tell me about an oil well on the property, that a big oil well had been discovered there, and the original well stood until they tore the old house down.

I then pointed toward my father, and told Johnny Hoell that he was raised on this land until he was ten years old, and that he was the only person still living among his family of nineteen siblings. "His name is Green Whitaker, and his father was Isaac," I said, needing him to know the history before his family came to be there.

I motioned for Johnny to get closer to say hello, but he reminded me of social distancing. "We don't have masks on."

"Right!" I said remembering.

He then acknowledged Dad with a nod. "Pleased to see you, Mr. Whitaker."

I thanked Mr. Hoell for allowing me to stand on the land. He acknowledged with a nod, another to my dad, smiled slightly and headed back toward the yellow house. I watched, standing there, not wanting to leave, feeling somehow planted. A feeling rushed from the earth through me and a well of emotion began to bubble and overflow inside and I wasn't sure why. After hearing the many stories over the years of the eighty acres, and the oil well down home, to see where the house sat in that bountiful expanse, filled me with tears and pride. For a moment I felt as if I were stepping back in time, and I imagined my family there, thriving. How my grandfather was forced to sell his land and the meaning of why the well was tapped was very clear.

Then I felt a new warmer and deep connection to Poppa Isaac, the man who had fathered my dad, to the land that fed them; and to the family who had cultivated and lived on it for many years. The rush of tears surprised me since I knew this was my singular experience, this connection that I felt in that moment. While trying to hide my tears, I couldn't try to explain it. What I felt in touching the ancestral lands, standing where my ancestors stood on the land that began before me. This land held a good portion of my history, my rooted tree's beginning, a history as solid as the earth beneath me, as vast as the cloudless blue sky above me.

All time and space disappeared. The generations between me, my father, and his, were suddenly connected by the warm grassy soil beneath my feet and swaths of green all around me. We were one. We are one. What they lived, learned, and gave us was broader shoulders, a wider open door, a shorter walk, and perhaps a coattail to help get your bearings. I walked where Poppa Isaac walked, where my nine-year-old Daddy had run, and played. The legacy of a father to his daughter is not just in a name but in the love he leaves and lives that spreads much wider than eighty acres or the big blue sky ever could.

Epilogue

Writing this book has been a love journey. I had the blessing of a great dad who I wanted to share with you, a gentle black father who walked with the grace of a country statesman and trusted counselor, who moved gently and spoke quietly behind the wisdom and quiet that lived on his face. His singing voice was the first I remember hearing. His arms always made little me feel safe and loved. His life is a testament to overcoming obstacles and looking for the light. His faith is an anchor, moral compass, and guiding light. And his southern sassy-styled wisdoms and musings have stayed with me, shepherding my path.

Until we get a rear-view look or become parents ourselves, we often don't realize at the time the importance of the gifts and lessons we learn or absorb from our parents. I've felt extraordinarily blessed at the childhood and life they gave me, and the values, kinship, and the love that I have known from them.

My dad raised us to be strong, brave women who didn't need a man for fulfillment; he wanted all my siblings to be people who were self-sufficient, kind, productive and virtuous in the world. His example engendered an expectation of service in us and he set that example by his own life, not just his words. Like his father had done for him. The hard-earned lessons he'd learned growing up black in the deep South often oppressed but never defeated showed us a solid work ethic of a man who lived deeply in his abiding faith at his very core. His history had dark places but there was always beauty between the lines, inside the walls, and outside the fields that tried to contain him. He is an archetypal father who was kind and protective and able to express his feelings. He emphasized the importance of family devotion and he showed up for all of us, teaching us how to show up for one another and for ourselves.

His hardly-spoken of dream to become a professional baseball player didn't dim his biggest dreams for us. We felt safe, loved and protected, a loving debt I can never repay. Each of us blossomed in our own ways from the light and love our parents gave. He trusted me and my siblings to be a representative of the family and to reflect the values they taught and lived at home and in the world: Be strong, love everybody, but don't let people walk over you; be kind and excellent in all things. And, remember who you are…God's child.

He walked in the cloth of pristine character and continues to teach us much of what he learned through his long glorious life. These lessons and stories were too rich to keep within. The old song says, "I said I wasn't gon' tell nobody but I couldn't keep it to myself!" In my mind, Dad earned his doctorate in the Sciences of Life and was a Professor of the highest calling.

Though ordinary in the sense of worldly accomplishments, my dad has lived an extraordinary life. A beloved soul and peacemaker, Dad's reach through our community is one of deference for the kind of person he is. The many lives he has touched, the way he cultivated and nurtured our family and so many others, leaves him revered and deeply loved. All the traditions, social mores, the life scars and lessons learned from his rural sharecropping boyhood certainly shaped the man he became, but gave him a precise and straightforward insight and wisdom for a better life, and laid the foundation for the father that he is. His story is not one of perfection, but a sharing, a "rev-el-ation" of a man I greatly admire.

A faithful husband, brother, uncle and friend, he showed me an example of excellence in a human doing life that has left a trail of insight and love. He taught us that simple can be great, and great can be simple. Never taking himself too seriously.

My dad's "success story" obviously isn't about money or fame. Rather, it's in the tenacity of his strength and love, wit and survival that his legacy is made. He perpetuated a cycle of love, despite being born into a time of hardship and hate. He carved space in a world that didn't always have room for him, not through outlandish heroic acts, but through being his authentic self and making all his decisions with a rare integrity, focused always on faith and family. That is his legacy. A legacy of love.

Acknowledgments

The journey this book began as a solo pilgrimage in my head but grew to incorporate so many people who surrounded me in finding the best way to tell this story. There was a grad student Rose (whose last name I can't recall) in a college English class who pulled me aside after I had submitted a paper for homework and said to me that I should write. Aside from song writing and some simple poetry I didn't think much of it in the busy of my young life. Having a couple of published articles in Inspired Woman magazine, that long ago planted seed took root when I met Jackie Parker whose writing workshop put me on a road of writing and stories, and how to share them. Her class was so eye opening and cathartic in my grief journey, but so necessary in my emotional and artistic growth. It is where I started writing my first book. Thank you for coming into my life and putting me on this journey.

The late Mr. Versie Jackson, my seventh-grade English teacher, gave me such a love of grammar and made learning it so much fun. And Ms. Paige in high school literature who put on music and instructed us to "write what you feel".

A gigantic thank you also to Jessica Swift, my editor for my first book *Finding My Voice: My Journey from Grief to Grace,* and helped me begin again with writing this book. You taught me so much about the process of fine tuning the words that poured out of my pen onto a page. I wish your expertise and guidance for every writer. You held my hand and helped me believe that I could do this kind of work sharing our stories, encouraging me all the way. I am still a work in process as a writer but I am so much better because of you. I learned from your excellent skills, your personal journey, and quick foul mouth wit. We've had some hard laughs, and some soft cries together and became good friends in the process. Big thanks to my editors Robert Yehling and the amazing Aviva Layton, who helped me smooth out the rough edges and really helped make this book so much better in big and small ways. Your input has been essential and invaluable for this book.

To my dearest treasured friend and sister Anika Noni Rose, thank you for writing such beautiful and impactful words of acknowledgment to Dad in the foreword. To all my family and the friends who've encouraged me to share what I was writing with a larger audience and to share my dad's stories with all of you, I thank you. Adam Aejaye Jackson, Sam Harris, Jackie Parker, my brilliant tea sisters, and my dearest Jenifer Lewis, each of you cheered me along the road to this book, I thank you all.

To my darling daughters, Skye and Liisi LaFontaine, who sat and listened again and again to chapters that I had written so that my words would have some audience. Thank you for making time to listen and gave honest feedback, especially during the pandemic when we all a bit crazy but had the time to do so. I hope you continue to learn from you grandfather's life lessons and mine, and that those gems can be a gift to your life. Your encouragement and engagement along the process meant so much.

And to my sweet love Scott Perkins, thank you for your excellent extra eyes and extra ears that helped me in the edits of this book journey. You have a great critical eye and a love of writing beyond the technical aspects you are called to. Thank you for all your great ideas, assistance, and understanding when my computer and I were inseparable. You're simply the best. More adventures await us, my love.

And Daddy, thank you for existing. For being such a great dad and good human expression of love. Parenting is an effort that changes as your children grow, and you mastered every stage. I can only tell our story from my point of view but the relationship you and I have is very special; certainly, my siblings all feel the same way. I am happy that I can share you with all the readers of this book, and they can get a glimpse of the wonderful man who raised and loved me. I hope they feel a little smarter and safer with some of your gems packed in their pockets. Your life has been a miracle and through this book, I hope more people fall in love with you the way your children do.

Keep on keeping on Daddy. I am grateful for every day I get to hear your voice, sit in your presence, have a conversation with you, and continue to learn from you. My root. My heart. My daddy.

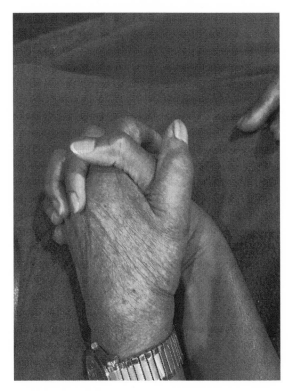

My Dad is still holding my hand

Jr. Scott, Mommy, Daddy, Alene, Kathy and me
(with the hair roller)

From left to right, Florece White, John Henry White, Earl White (and baby
son), (Mudea) Lois White, Daddy, great grandmother Mamma Hattie Osby,
Kathy, Doris White and me (with the hair shot)
Some of our maternal family members.

Young W.T.Whitaker later renamed Zach

Jr. in his bedroom playing his stereo

Big Chain Grocery and Cafeteria anchored the
south end of the new shopping center located on
the corner of Line Avenue and Pierremont Road

The restaurant where our family dined some Sundays

Dad in a fancy jacket in our almost modern kitchen on 73ʳᵈ street

A lane bearing the Whitaker family name in Holly

Whitaker Lane in Holly

A young Green, with the "Mary Evergreen Spiritual

The gospel singing group Dad was a part of and managed for twenty one years. Two of his brothers were also in it, Uncle Leroy top left and Zach lower right.

Daddy and his youngest brother Zach Whitaker

Green and his kids, from left to right Green Jr., Nita, Dad, Kathy, Alene, and Uncle Dave

Green and his grands, JeRelle, Liisi, Jamerrio, Dad, Skye, Jamar and Uncle Dave

Green's big beautiful family! From left to right, Nephews Jamar and Jamer-rio, Scott(Nita's husband), Nita, Kathy, Dad, Jr. Bryce (Alene's husband), Alene, Nita's daughter Skye, niece JeRelle, Uncle Dave (Dad's brother), and Liisi (Nita's daughter)

Dad and Me

Made in the USA
Middletown, DE
25 May 2022